From Unsure To Secure

FROM unsure TO SECURE

6 SIMPLE STEPS
TO SECURING YOUR
FINANCIAL FUTURE SO
YOU CAN MAKE MORE,
BE MORE, AND LIVE MORE

VANDY VERMA

NEW YORK

LONDON • NASHVILLE • MELBOURNE • VANCOUVER

From Unsure to Secure

6 Simple Steps to Securing Your Financial Future So You Can Make More, Be More, and Live More

© 2021 Vandy Verma

Published in New York, New York, by Morgan James Publishing in partnership with Difference Press. Morgan James is a trademark of Morgan James, LLC. www.MorganJamesPublishing.com

ISBN 9781642799965 paperback
ISBN 9781642799972 eBook
ISBN 9781642799989 audiobook
Library of Congress Control Number: 2020933239

Cover Design by:
Chris Treccani
www.3dogcreative.net

Interior Design by:
Christopher Kirk
www.GFSstudio.com

Editor:
Nkechi Obi

Book Coaching:
The Author Incubator

Morgan James is a proud partner of Habitat for Humanity Peninsula and Greater Williamsburg. Partners in building since 2006.

Get involved today! Visit
MorganJamesPublishing.com/giving-back

*Dedicated to my husband, who said to me,
"Don't search. Dig."*

Table of Contents

CHAPTER 1:

Sidelines Aren't Where You Belong

Take a deep breath and give yourself a pat on the back for deciding to read a book on such a dull topic! I mean, why read a book on financial security when fiction, romance, or mystery are the alternative options, right?

On a slightly serious note, by taking the time to read a book like this one, you have established that you are a problem-solver. When issues arise, you most likely are *not* someone who sits by the sidelines; instead, you are someone who takes matters in their own hands, takes action, and actively participates in solving the problem.

Well, in that case, I'd like to start off by saying congratulations! You have already taken the initial steps to achieve whatever it is that you are trying to achieve. It takes a tremendous amount of courage to be honest with yourself and to recognize that you are struggling or not happy with your circumstances or maybe just want to work on making things better than they currently are.

That is the first, and certainly the most crucial step in the process. Reaching out for help is the hardest part, yet here you are. When we are confronted with difficulties, we are usually able to persevere and succeed, but sometimes, we can use an outside perspective. Gaining insights from someone else's journey, similar to our own, could be very useful. That's where I come in; if you feel stuck or frustrated, then I know how you feel. I've been there.

My financial situation wasn't where I had expected it to be. In fact, it was in flux. Worries about my family's financial security kept me up at night. The thought that kept repeating in my head over and over was "How can I make more money at work and secure my family's future?"

Maybe you are in a similar situation. You are not where you'd hoped to be, maybe because you are stuck in a dead-end job. Or maybe life has thrown an expected curveball of a medical illness that has now become a financial drain. Or maybe you are unsure about your financial future in light of your unexpected divorce. Or maybe nothing is wrong, but there is a nagging urge that is telling you there's more inside of you. You are raring to get to the next level in your career and life. Whatever the reason, the bottom line is you are not looking to settle; you want more.

Wouldn't it be nice to have a crystal ball?

A way to see what the future looks like?

With everything that is going on in the world lately, things certainly don't feel secure. Industries getting disrupted, jobs getting displaced, big behemoth brand names that had dominated the marketplace for decades biting the dust. It seems there is no such thing as financial security anymore. The future seems precarious. The only sense of security you can feel is in the tangible income you bring home, and the only way to feel more secure about the future is to have more of it. Making more money has never felt more important and urgent.

This lack of security feels unsettling and heavy. And this heaviness could feel like a cloud that hangs over you that won't let up no matter what you do. You want to feel secure. This constant pressure could be causing a strain on your relationships and overall lifestyle. It may be hard for you to switch off the worries and enjoy time with your friends and family. Simple things that made your life feel normal like spending quality time with your kids, going on date nights, taking casual walks, going to the movies or the gym or simply watching your favorite shows are on hold because the problem-solving side of you wants a resolution before you can go out and do any of that or fully enjoy anything.

You are determined to see the light at the end of this tunnel because then you will be able to enjoy your relationships more and feel happy and relaxed when you spend time with family and friends, not absent-minded and stressed. You would be able to take care of your health as well, something that has slipped on your list of priorities. You look forward to going on vacations and recharging your batteries. You cannot wait to get out of the situation you are in. You dream of a future where you have solved all your problems-when all this is behind you, your financial worries have vanished, and you have reached the next level at work and the next chapter in your life!

As someone who has seen the light at the end of the tunnel and has gone from feeling *unsure* about the future to feeling *secure*, I can now confidently say that this journey you have embarked upon to create a better tomorrow is in your control, and everything that you are wishing and dreaming of is possible.

You've got this!

CHAPTER 2:

Why Me?

I was angry, so angry!

At myself, at the situation, at everything.

To provide a quick background around the time of the incident, I'd worked in corporate America most of my adult life; my husband, however, had been an entrepreneur who had owned multiple businesses. One of his business investments, a restaurant my husband had recently bought as a way for us to grow financially, had turned out to be a nightmare!

The previous owner had led us to believe that the restaurant was a potential "goldmine." He was a great salesperson who had reeled us in with a very convincing story.

He'd said that the restaurant had an impressive sales record and a loyal customer following, and the only reason he was walking away from it was that he was looking to retire. He further convinced us that with a new owner who was more hands-on and engaged, the sales could increase drastically. We bought into the lovely story and the promise.

What was massively downplayed in the story was that even though the sales were great, the expenses were greater. We very quickly found out that there were way too many hidden expenses in the restaurant. These expenses were so big that they not only swallowed all the revenue but also forced us to put money into the business from our pocket every month to keep the restaurant running. The expenses were huge; we had to tap into our savings. And soon, I watched in horror helplessly as over a decade's worth of our hard-earned savings vanished into this money pit in a matter of months.

The savings we'd set aside for our kids' college, for our retirement-all gone!

I asked myself,

"How did this happen?"

"Why us?"

"What did we do wrong?"

And because I'm someone who takes full responsibility for my life, I disappointedly asked myself,

"How could I let this happen?"

"How could I be so irresponsible?"

"What was I thinking?"

My mind was flooded with questions.

Questions that tormented me.

Questions I didn't have the answers to.

I blamed myself profusely.

My husband was going through the same experience, and even though we were in this together, I somehow let this loss affect *me* on a deep, personal level. This experience shattered my belief that I was a level-headed and intelligent person who could make sound decisions. I internalized this failure. It felt like it was not the business that had failed, I had failed. I had failed in being a good partner to my husband and a responsible parent to my children. It was a huge blow to my confidence.

After having spent a lot of time in what I'd like to call a "blame and shame" phase, blaming myself and everyone involved and feeling ashamed for being in the situation we were in, the problem-solving side of me kicked in. I decided that I needed to do my share to help us get out of this situation. I needed to find a way to make more money, a *lot* more money, to get myself and my family out of the mess we'd landed ourselves into. I had to find a solution to this problem. I began furiously scanning for growth opportunities at work.

To my utter disappointment, there were no open positions in my workplace that I could grow into. At the time, I worked as a designer, and the corporate structure of the company I worked for was relatively flat. There were no immediate positions of growth. There were a few management and leadership positions that I could aspire to grow into with enough time and experience, but none that were open at the time. There was no clear path to getting to the next level.

I felt stuck. I didn't know what to do. There was no imminent hope for a promotion, yet I didn't have the luxury of simply sticking around and waiting.

I just had to find a way.

What followed after this phase was a life-changing journey. A journey filled with growth, learning, unlearning, *aha* moments, roller coaster of emotions, transformative experiences, etc. etc.

Fast forward a few years. I grew by leaps and bounds, ended up getting promoted multiple times in my company to positions that were specifically created for my role to finally reach a senior leadership position while creating a life and career I love in the process. I don't say this to impress you. I say this to impress *upon* you to never ever let lack of opportunities dampen the fire in your belly. Know that you have the power to create opportunities even when they don't exist.

You have a lot more power than you think you do!

CHAPTER 3:

You Were Born to Be a L.E.A.D.E.R.

I t is my privilege to be in a position today where people seek my guidance and ask me to mentor them. My journey of growth intrigues them. They often ask me to reveal important, actionable details-to give them nuggets of wisdom, the practical insights I have gained over the course of my career and life. It brings me great joy and a sense of fulfillment when I'm able to share the lessons I've learned with anyone who is willing to truly listen and do the work of applying them. So, writing a book about it just made sense.

I have written this book as a well-thought-out plan that has the potential to move the needle and deliver results. It was important to me that this book is *not* just a bunch of words that may make you feel good now but don't mean much in the long run. Therefore, the book in its earlier chapters is focused on the "big picture"-the knowledge and the strategies-before zooming in on the details, the tactics, and the actionable items in the following chapters. Finally, it illustrates how to apply all those strategies and tactics into real-life situations to get the desired results.

In this book, *I have taken the "less is more" approach* and have focused only on the *big* ideas that can bring you maximum impact, instead of giving you a million little tips or nuggets of information that may have little to no impact in the long run. One of the most important things that I've learned to appreciate in business and life is the value of *not* dabbling. When you dabble, you remain on a shallow level, and for any lasting change to occur, you need to go deep and master the craft.

Even though we may not want to hear this, there *really* are no quick fixes or shortcuts to any kind of success. This is the reason crash diets don't work in the long run. Much has been written lately about how losing weight too quickly, like any sudden change to your body, is dangerous. Crash diets, diet pills, and fasting indeed induce rapid weight loss; however, they also cause you to lose muscle mass and may injure the heart and other vital organs in the process. Instead of aiming for an overnight miracle (quick fix), it makes greater sense to opt for a sensible nutritious eating plan as well as a realistic exercise regimen. This is a long-term and sustainable approach. This book takes the same approach-a dependable, sustainable and long-term approach to success in business and in life.

The idea of writing a book forced me to reflect on my growth in a very concrete way. I needed to be very clear on what the exact factors were that helped fuel my success. So, after reflecting deeply on the entire process and retracing my steps, I narrowed the process down to six major steps, each one of them crucial for success. The framework I devised incorporates all the elements that are essential to make lasting changes, and I crafted an acronym for it called the L.E.A.D.E.R. framework.

In crafting this acronym, it is *not* my intention to define the essence of a leader or leadership. That's *not* where I'm going with this. What I *have* done here is outlined all the steps that will lead you to massive and continuous growth. And such growth will not only bring you financial success, but it will also bring out the leader in you in the process. Leadership at its core is not about leading others; it's essentially about leading only one person to a better place, and that person is yourself. When you lead yourself towards something actively and consistently, sooner or later, people around you will begin to take notice; your journey might inspire them, and then out of their free will they might choose to follow you. That is true leadership. By taking charge of your growth and acting on these steps, you are bound to become a leader of your own life as well as someone who others look up to. That evolution will just be an obvious by-product of the process.

Here's what the acronym stands for:

L: Learn

E: Execute

A: Accelerate

D: Deliver

E: Evaluate

R: Rejoice!

L: Learn

In this step, you will discover the reason why you are stuck and how to make progress, and you will explore what I consider to be one of the biggest leverages human beings have: the power of knowledge.

E: Execute

In this step, you will discuss the idea that knowledge is power; however, it is only potential power until activated, which means knowledge is useless until acted upon. So, we will discuss the tangible steps that you can take to start applying the knowledge in your life. A formidable combination of knowledge and action is the primary driver of success.

A: Accelerate

In this step, you will learn how to build momentum and optimize and accelerate success. You will also learn how to pre-empt potential obstacles that might show up and sabotage your momentum and how to prevent them from doing so.

D: Deliver

In this step, we will examine not only how to increase your value (and income eventually) but also find ways to tactically deliver it.

E: Evaluate

In this step, you will learn to reflect and evaluate the process and outcomes of what worked and what didn't and use this knowledge to improve going forward and/or to course correct.

R: Rejoice!

If I had to pick a favorite of all the steps, I would choose this one. This step demonstrates how happiness has a massive influence on success and how being happy significantly increases your chances of being successful.

While the steps are laid out sequentially in this acronym, they do not necessarily need to occur in a sequence. In fact, they could often occur simultaneously and out of order-for example, learning while evaluating or accelerating while executing. Try to think of these steps as different instruments in an orchestra. They might all play together at once sometimes, but at other times, there may be only one or two instruments playing, and there is no hierarchy or sequence either.

It brings me great joy and satisfaction to see people thrive by taking the initiative of acting on these steps. It warms my heart to see them apply these ageless philosophies and create lasting change in their careers and lives. The concrete insights I share in this book have enabled me to take massive action and bring financial success in my own life.

These six steps cover the timeless principles that helped me get from a position of feeling helpless to empowered, from seeing little to no opportunities to achieving massive growth both financially and personally. I feel privileged to be in a position that allows me to live a happy and fulfilled life while serving others and helping them become better versions of themselves.

It is my honor to share the L.E.A.D.E.R. framework with you!

CHAPTER 4:

Let's Try a Different Way (L: Learn)

Why are You Stuck?

> *"Insanity is repeating the same steps over and over and expecting a different result."*
> – Albert Einstein

Isn't December fun? It's a time of festivity, a time to celebrate and have fun with loved ones. It's also a time to start thinking of the new year. The idea of a new year brings a feeling of *hope*. With the upcoming year, people feel like they will be given a blank slate, a chance to start

15

over, to correct past missteps, and to do things right and get their lives in order. Time to make new resolutions.

One of the most popular New Year's resolutions for a lot of people is to lose weight and get in shape. Cash registers cannot stop ringing in gyms in January as people are tripping over themselves to sign up for annual memberships.

"Things will be different this time. I'll be good and follow through. It'll be great!" they promise themselves enthusiastically.

And things *are* different and great!

For twenty-three days, seventeen hours, and six minutes. Approximately.

Often by the time February approaches, life starts to get in the way-

"too busy,"

"no time,"

"too tired."

As the list of excuses starts to become bigger, the crowds in the gyms start to become smaller. The new members start to fall back into their old habits. This is a classic example of what it means to repeat the same steps over and over and expect a different result.

New Year.

New resolution.

Old steps.

Old results.

The moral of the story is simple: if you want a different result, you need to take different steps. If you are stuck and are wondering why, chances are you have been repeating the same steps as well. Maybe you are trying to get to the next level at work by working harder than before or putting in longer hours or taking on more, but they are essentially more of the same steps you've taken before. The approach is not new. And here's the thing: nothing changes if nothing changes.

So, in order to break through this pattern and make progress, you will have to be *open* to new ideas and willing to try a different way of doing things even if it feels uncomfortable or counterintuitive. If you want something you've never had, you'll have to do something you've never done.

Empty Your Cup

> *"It ain't what you don't know that gets you into trouble. It's what you know for sure that just ain't so."*
> – Mark Twain

This section of the book is about learning; however, before you dive deep into learning mode, it is important to empty your cup.

Empty your cup?

"What does that mean?" you ask.

Here's the story …

Once upon a time, there was a wise Zen master. People traveled from far away to seek his help. On this particular day, a scholar came to visit the master to inquire about Zen. The Zen master served tea. He poured his visitor's cup full and then kept on pouring. The tea overflowed onto the table, onto the floor. The scholar watched the overflow until he no longer could restrain himself.

"Stop! The cup is full already. Can't you see?" the scholar exclaimed.

"Exactly," the Zen master replied with a smile.

"You are like this cup.

So full of ideas that nothing more will fit in.

In order to learn, you need to first empty your cup."

I like the "empty your cup" story a lot because it is a great reminder that in order to learn we have to be humble and empty our minds to make room for the new. This is exactly what needed to happen to me at the outset of my transformative journey. In order to learn and make any significant change in my life, I had to first *unlearn* a few ludicrous lies that I thought were truths. I call them "Garbage Ideas" because by the time we are adults, our minds are full of many ideas, beliefs, and notions that we consider to be true when the reality is a lot of them are simply not true. When you hear a lie over and over enough times, it becomes the truth. Therefore, in order to fill our minds with valuable, life-changing insights, we need to first make room for them by taking out the garbage.

Garbage Idea #1: Courage Means Fearlessness

It felt like my heart was in my throat, throbbing violently.

The large conference hall I was standing in was packed with strangers.

I was in a foreign country where I'd just attended a three-day-long workshop. It was a workshop on marketing and branding with an over-arching focus on authenticity and human psychology. I had a lot of "light bulb moments" throughout this workshop. A lot of my notions about human psychology that I knew to be true were challenged and many myths debunked. And now, on the fourth day, I was amidst a large crowd attending a bigger event, which was sort of a grand finale to the workshop.

Standing in this sea of people, my face was flushed, and my body was numb. Every part of my body seemed paralyzed except for my right arm that seemed to have a mind of its own as it slowly raised itself. This was my response to the event presenter's question,

"Would anyone like to share their experience with the workshop they just attended?"

You see, any other time of my life I would not even consider offering an unrehearsed speech in front of a large crowd (that sounds crazy!), but this time was different.

I had acquired a different perspective on *courage* in the last few days, something that would change my life forever.

Up until that point in my life, I had lived with this notion that having courage meant having no fear, and the people who were "courageous" were different from the others. They simply didn't experience fear. This is what allowed them to do "scary" things like perform in front of a camera, talk to complete strangers, jump out of planes, do adventurous things, and possibly the scariest of all, speak in public. In a way, they had an "unfair advantage" over others. This is what I believed to be true.

And then, I was given life-changing insight at this recent workshop. I learned that "courage is *not* the absence of fear; it is the ability to act in the face of fear." So, even the most courageous people have fear. They just take action despite their fear.

"Wait, what?! Are you saying, fear is normal and that anybody can be courageous?" I remember thinking this to myself during the workshop as this new notion hit me like a brick (in a good way).

"Wow, that changes everything!" I thought, feeling ecstatic as my mind slowly opened up to a whole new world of possibilities.

Before this revelation, I thought fear was a *bad* thing because being fearful was a sign of weakness. Being fearful meant you weren't as strong as the other "fearless" people; therefore, attempting scary things was not exactly an option because fear would block your path every time. But that was about to change, starting with that very moment.

In that moment, my curiosity became bigger than my fear. I was curious to see if what I'd just learned about courage was indeed true. I was going to do something despite feeling unprepared, despite being afraid. I was going to give that unrehearsed speech in front of a huge crowd. I was going to feel the fear and do it anyway!

To give you some background, public speaking was not exactly my forte back then. Okay, I'll say it-I was petrified of it! I'm not sure how and when the fear of public speaking had set in. Maybe I had a negative experience during my childhood, or maybe there was another reason; regardless, the point is the fear was there, and because I had never spoken in front of such a large audience before, even the thought scared me. I was terrified to do it this time as well, but I decided to go for it anyway. Besides, considering that I was somewhere in the outskirts of London, a part of me said, *"The crowd here is British, with your mixed foreign accent, they won't understand half the things you say anyway, so you really can't screw this up."*

The speaker spotted me with my hand up and asked me to come up on stage to share. What happened in the next few minutes felt a bit surreal. It's as if time had slowed down. Everything seemed to operate in slow motion. All sounds merged into one big incoherent blob. I got up on stage, took the microphone, and started speaking. I don't remember much of what I said, but I do remember this: to my utter disbelief, it felt fairly easy to speak. The words seemed to flow out of my mouth. Not sure how. I was simply speaking from the heart. And even though hundreds of pairs of eyes were peering at me, they all seemed a bit "out of focus" to me. In those few precious moments, nothing mattered anymore-the fear was gone!

The lesson that I learned that has been repeated in my life over and over since then is that courage does not mean fearlessness. As long as there is life, there will be fear.

No one is fearless. Period.

Courageous people just do one thing differently in the face of fear: they carry on. That's the only difference. The fear is still there, but they override it with action. I call this a life-changing insight because once I learned that fear is natural and I stopped getting frustrated with it or wishing for it to go away, I could do more things that felt uncomfortable like trying new and unfamiliar things, engaging in necessary but difficult conversations with people, learning new skills, and so on.

Now, if you happen to be someone who is a natural at public speaking, you might not understand why it could be a big deal for anyone. I get it. But here's the thing, we are all naturally brave in certain areas in life and not so brave in others. For instance, I'm terrified of roller coasters. Yup, total chicken! But I'm not afraid to speak my mind even when my thinking is different from the crowd.

I don't bite my tongue to fit in. On the other hand, someone could be a daredevil when it comes to rollercoasters but could hold back their opinion when it's different than the pack so as to please others and not ruffle any feathers. To be clear, there is no judgment here, just an acknowledgment that every single person faces fear. If you have a pulse, you have fear.

It doesn't matter what that thing is that you're afraid of. What matters is that you realize that being afraid is a natural thing that everyone faces. The only thing you need to do in the face of fear is to take action, and soon enough, the fear will dissipate. Being courageous not only helps you grow as a person, but it also brings a sense of freedom. The biggest thing that holds people back is fear. Once you realize that fear can be overcome anytime, it can become a complete game-changer. Ever since gaining this life-changing insight about courage, I consistently take more and more action in the face of fear (still do), doing things that feel uncomfortable. For example, free jumping fifty feet into a waterfall from a cliff or walking on burning coals weren't things I was comfortable with, but I did them anyway.

"Be comfortable with the uncomfortable" became my mantra. And what I learned on the way was that finding the courage to step outside of your comfort zone can be hard, so very hard at times, and courage can be more perishable than strawberries. The fact that I can muster up the courage to get on the treadmill and run today, where I have to push myself, does not guarantee that the courage will be there tomorrow. I'll have to muster it up again and run anyway.

Fighting your fears will be a constant battle, but it *does* get easier with repetition. The more you get used to doing uncomfortable things, the easier it gets to do them. The fear, the discomfort will be there; it just becomes easier to overcome it with time. In fact, interestingly, some of the fears could actually become great sources of passion. For instance, as I shared earlier, there was a time when I was very uncomfortable with public speaking, but now I love it! Love it so much that the idea actually excites and invigorates me.

If you too want to accelerate your growth, actively seek to do things that you are afraid of or at least that make you uncomfortable. By doing so, you will train your mind to get used to feeling the fear and moving past it. Slowly and steadily, your courage muscle will grow and expand, and then, when you are faced with a situation that requires you to step up and be brave, courage will be there.

More Validation: Real Life Hero's Thoughts on Fear

I didn't want to blink or breathe as I watched a larger-than-life American hero speak.

I was in Vegas attending a business conference when I had the incredible honor to meet and learn from Robert O'Neill, the navy seal who fired the shots that killed Osama

Bin Laden! He was also on the mission that rescued Captain Phillips during the Somalian pirate crisis. He is a true real-life hero-someone who is an embodiment of bravery and courage.

I was simply awestruck as I watched him share firsthand, jaw-dropping accounts of his missions. During a part of his speech, when talking about his missions, he said people often ask him, "Weren't you afraid?" To that his response was, "Yes, I was. So what? It's okay to be afraid because fear is natural. Without fear, there won't be any courage." Well, there you have it. If a real-life hero says fear is natural, then there's a lot of hope for the rest of humanity.

Courage is a muscle. You can grow and expand it by repeatedly facing your fears, i.e. doing uncomfortable things regularly. So that means there is nothing standing in between you and abundant courage, correct? Not quite. There is something that will block your path every time you want to step outside your comfort zone. And that thing is-your brain!

Your Brain Is Not as Smart as You Think

Your brain has one job, and that is to keep you alive.

Every single second of your life, it is working diligently to keep you safe. It is constantly scanning for threats and giving you commands to act appropriately. The reason you don't consider walking in front of moving traffic or you instantly retract your hand when it touches something hot is because your brain is working for you. This is a very useful feature of the brain-something that has helped humans survive since the beginning of time. In prehistoric times, a rustle in the bushes could mean a saber-toothed tiger was approaching, so the brain would instinctively put you in a survival mode, and your body would immediately go into a *flight or fight* mode, both of which would be very useful in keeping you alive.

However, as humans and their surroundings evolved, there is one thing that didn't evolve at the same pace, and that thing is the brain. In today's day and age, there are no saber-toothed tigers or other predators; in fact, there are barely any factors that threaten the survival of human beings. We live in a time when life is safer and more comfortable than it has ever been; however, the human brain continues to operate at the same level of threat alert. Any experience that is unknown or unfamiliar or one where the outcome is not predictable appears as a threat to your brain, and it reacts in the same way as it would to a predator. With your brain's hypervigilant tendency and overzealous attitude of wanting to keep you alive, it has created a phenomenon we commonly refer to as "The Comfort Zone."

Anything that is known and familiar to you has been filed as a "safe" experience by your brain, and it becomes a part of your comfort zone. Your brain allows you to have such an experience without feeling uncomfortable or afraid. However, try having an experience that is *not* known or familiar to your brain, and your brain will instantly go into high alert mode and start to make you feel uncomfortable or fearful. For instance, speaking to a close friend or your spouse about routine stuff is within your comfort zone; you more or less can predict the nature of the conversation, and therefore, it's within your comfort zone. However, speaking up in a meeting to voice your opinion, especially if it's a new idea that has not been discussed in the past, could feel very uncomfortable because there are many unknown variables and unpredictable outcomes to such an event. You risk disapproval from your peers; you risk being ridiculed or judged. Such a thing could be very stressful. This feeling of discomfort is the result of stepping outside of your comfort zone and your brain signaling you to stop and go back into your comfort zone because it thinks you are going to die.

Your comfort zone is a space where you feel safe and secure because everything inside of it is known and familiar; there, the patterns are predictable. Comfort zones are comfortable, for sure; however, there is only one problem with them: people don't grow in them!

Growth and comfort zones are mutually exclusive. Whenever you attempt to do anything new or unfamiliar, your mind sees it as a threat and immediately makes you feel emotionally and physically uncomfortable. You can feel your subconscious mind pulling you back toward your comfort zone each time you try something new. Even thinking about doing something different from what you're accustomed to will make you feel tense and uneasy. Your brain signal is telling you, "Stop ... don't do this. We are going to die!"

One such drastic life change that I experienced that catapulted me *way* outside of my comfort zone was when I went to college for the first time. I had had a very sheltered childhood. I had been a Daddy's girl, and my mom was always there for me, taking care of all my needs. And now that I had to move out for the first time in my life at the age of seventeen, I had to do everything by myself. I was on my own. From getting used to living in a new city to negotiating apartment leases, doing laundry, buying furniture, learning how to cook, managing finances-the list goes on-everything was outside of my comfort zone at first. I remember being overwhelmed and terribly homesick at times, but in the grand scheme of things, I can see how that was also a period of extreme growth. By repeatedly doing things that felt uncomfortable at first, I eventually grew up and became an adult in the process.

Stepping out of the comfort zone can be very scary at times, but for growth to occur, it must be done. If you want to continue to grow, you must try to learn new things, gain different experiences, or open yourself to diverse perspectives. This is the reason high achievers are always stretching themselves, pushing themselves out of their comfort zones.

They are very aware of how quickly the comfort zone, in any area, becomes a rut. They know that complacency is the great enemy of creativity and future possibilities. For you to grow, to get out of your comfort zone, you have to be willing to feel awkward and uncomfortable doing new things the first few times. If it's worth doing well, it's worth doing poorly until you get a feel for it, until you develop a new comfort zone at a new, higher level of competence. For instance, I began my career as a fashion designer; my primary job was to design apparel. I had a strong skillset for it that I had developed in college, as well as out of my passion for design. I loved it!

So, quite obviously, I created a very comfortable zone with the whole experience. However, as my career progressed and I eventually found myself in management and leadership positions, my old skill set became somewhat irrelevant. In order to be successful, I needed a whole new set of skills: people management skills, critical thinking, communication skills, team-building skills, etc., etc. Every time I would be faced with a new challenge or hit a bump in the road, my brain would make me so uncomfortable. There were times when my brain would tell me to go back into my comfort zone of doing things I knew like the back of my hand and could do in my sleep. But my brain was wrong and was giving me bad advice. Staying in my comfort zone would've been an easy choice, but it would've kept me playing small in my career.

Garbage Idea #2: Talent Is the Mother of Skill

All my life I had heard things like:

"She's a born singer."

"He can't dance. He has two left feet."

"He's a natural athlete."

"I'm not a creative person."

And oftentimes, more abstract versions like:

"She's got *it*!" or "He's got *it*!"

This led me to believe that *"it"* was the reason these people were good at something. Their natural talent was the only reason why people were skilled at anything. So, I was led to believe that talent was the mother of skill.

Every person was innately talented at certain things, and they had a certain amount of intelligence that was (more or less) fixed. You either were a good singer, or you weren't. You either were a smart person, or you weren't. There was no third option.

So, with that mindset, I just accepted that I am inherently good at certain things; for example, I realized from an early age that I loved to design things, so any creative project, no matter how difficult or laborious, did not faze me.

However, there were other things that I believed I could *not* be good at, so *I didn't even try!* For example, I saw myself as a creative person; however, I didn't think of writing as one of my strengths, and I most definitely didn't see myself as an author. So, the thought of writing a book did not cross my mind for an overwhelming majority of my life-four decades plus, to be specific. I thought for someone to be an author, it meant the person came out of their mother's womb with a pen clutched in one hand and a degree in literature in the other, and their first words were not "ma-ma" or "da-da;" they were *"To be or not to be."*

Authors were just born with books inside of them. Therefore, I was convinced that no one could *become* an author; they either were, or they weren't.

Enter Carol Dweck, the knight in shining armor who saved me from this preposterous lie!

Dweck's work provided me with life-changing insight on the difference between the "fixed" mindset and the "growth" mindset. Carol Dweck is a researcher at Stanford University best known for her work on "the fixed mindset versus the growth mindset." She introduced these ideas and wrote a book to describe each mindset in more detail. Here's how Dweck describes the difference between these two mindsets and how they impact your performance:

"In a fixed mindset, students believe their basic abilities, their intelligence, their talents, are just fixed traits. They have a certain amount and that's that, and then their goal becomes to look smart all the time and never look dumb. In a growth mindset, students understand that their talents and abilities can be developed through effort, good teaching, and persistence. They don't necessarily think

everyone's the same or anyone can be Einstein, but they believe everyone can get smarter if they work at it."

At a fleeting glance, the concept may seem similar to the age-old concept of "nature versus nurture," but upon closer inspection, it becomes apparent that it is much deeper than that, and it has a lot more layers to it. People in a *fixed* mindset believe you are born with a fixed level of intelligence that cannot be modified. You either are or aren't good at something based on your inherent nature because it's just who you are. People in a *growth* mindset believe their abilities and intelligence can be developed with effort, learning, and persistence. Their basic abilities are simply a starting point for their potential. They don't believe everyone is the same, but they hold onto the idea that everyone can become smarter if they try. *The fixed mindset is the most common and the most damaging,* so it's worth understanding and considering how it's affecting you.

In a fixed mindset, you believe "I'm just not good at dancing." In a growth mindset, you believe "Anyone can be good at anything. Skill comes only from effort and practice. I can be good at dancing if I put my mind to it." *People with a fixed mindset believe failure is devastating* and will try to avoid failure as much as possible. If a person believes "I'm not a natural athlete," then when they face any kind of failure, for example, while learning a new sport, their mind will tell them, *"This is not your thing. You're not good at this. Don't waste your time. Give up now."* People with a growth mindset believe failure or setbacks are just important pieces of feedback in the learning process. So, when faced with setbacks or failures, they adjust their level of effort or approach. For example, in the same case of learning a new sport, they will adjust their strategy or technique, get a coach, and practice more, but they won't give up. This subtle difference in mindset changes the trajectory of success.

Dweck's research has demonstrated that people who have a growth mindset are more likely to grow and maximize their potential. They tend to take on more risks and challenges and learn from criticism rather than ignoring it. They are inspired by the success of others rather than feeling threatened by it. When people believe they can get better and smarter and when they realize that their effort has an effect on their success, they put in extra time, leading to higher achievement, success, and growth.

Let's look at a few key areas where this difference in mindset becomes very distinctive:

Challenges

In a *fixed* mindset, you want to hide your flaws, so you're not judged or labeled a failure. People with a fixed mindset avoid challenges because it makes them feel like they're not talented or smart. You stick with what you know to keep up your confidence.

In a *growth* mindset, your flaws are just a to-do list of things to improve. Those with a growth mindset seek and thrive on challenges. They want to stretch themselves because they know that they will grow and learn. "This is hard but so much fun!"

Setbacks

In a *fixed* mindset, setbacks and failures define you. As was the case with me and the restaurant failing. I had a fixed mindset back then, so to me the restaurant had not failed, *I had failed*.

In a *growth* mindset, failures are temporary setbacks. You look at the setback simply as an event and don't let it forever define your intelligence, abilities, or character.

Effort

People with a *fixed* mindset believe that success should be won without effort-that you're born with natural talents and abilities. For instance, if you're romantically compatible with someone, you should share all the same views, and everything should just come naturally.

Those with a *growth* mindset believe the opposite; you have to work hard in order to achieve success-it doesn't just come naturally. They believe a lasting relationship comes from effort and working through inevitable differences.

Outcomes

In a *fixed* mindset, it's all about the outcome. If you fail, you think all your effort was wasted.

In a *growth* mindset, it's all about the process because you're applying yourself, giving your best, and solving challenging and important problems. It's about the journey, not just the destination. As a result, even if the outcome is not a "success," you feel the effort was rewarding and worthwhile in itself. People with the growth mindset stretch themselves more, think bigger, take more risks, and learn something new, regardless of the outcome.

This simple yet brilliant insight opened up a whole new world for me. My life changed. When I realized that I could acquire new skills and grow and become better at practically anything. I started to look at all areas in my work and life that I previously felt I wasn't good at as possibilities for growth. I started to take on more risks and challenges and put in the time and effort to learn and become better. This mindset shift fueled my growth significantly. For instance, as I mentioned earlier in this chapter, with my old *fixed mindset,* I didn't think of writing as one of my strengths or see myself as an author. However, with the new perspective on *growth mindset,* I now believed that I could learn new skills and become good at anything I put my mind and enough effort into. So, when I decided to write a book, I became obsessed with the idea to learn and become better with practice. I read books and articles on how to write, watched podcasts and interviews of authors where they shared their writing journey, the challenges they faced, and how they overcame them, practiced a lot, wrote and wrote and wrote, solicited feedback on my writing and used it to improve, and finally, to accelerate my growth, I hired a book coach who showed me the ropes of how to write a book using the right strategies and techniques.

The journey that led me to finish writing this book has probably been one of the hardest things I've done in my life. I had to overcome massive amounts of discomfort and fear with every step I took towards the finish line. The voice in my head would say things like,

"Who do you think you are?"

"You're not a writer."

"People who've written books have had decades of experience. They were experts,"

or *"No one's going to read your book."*

"You will need to do tons of research to even produce something worthwhile,"

and blah, blah, blah.

While writing this book, there hardly were any moments where I felt comfortable or felt that things were in my control. In fact, discomfort, also known as fear, was my constant companion. It would show up in many different forms, such as hesitation, doubt, awkwardness, procrastination, or perfectionism. I would second-guess my decision of writing a book. I would doubt if I was competent enough to write.

In hindsight, I can see that it was simply my brain trying to keep me in the *fixed mindset* zone, stopping me from attempting something new and challenging. And yet, the reality is by continuing to take action despite the challenges, by putting one foot in front of the other, I *did* become an author! And I *did* finish a book that is being read by people (you are doing it right now).

This becoming proficient at something unfamiliar can absolutely be the case for you too. Know that you can become better at anything as long as you are willing to put in enough time and effort and are willing to persevere during the process. And because there is no ceiling to your improvement, you can learn and grow continuously. It's good to know that these are not just some feel-good words from a motivational speech. I not only know this to be the truth from many of my own experiences, but it's also comforting that this idea is actually backed by scientific research.

If there is one thing that I want to scream from the rooftops, it is this:

You have unlimited potential! And there is no limit to how much you can learn and grow.

So now that you know the difference between "growth mindset" and "fixed mindset" and how they can affect success, it would be very useful to know how to have more of a growth mindset. In order to shape the mindset, we need to look into the mind.

Don't Mind the Brain

Let's talk about the mind and the brain for a moment.

The brain and mind are not the same. The brain is part of the visible, tangible organ inside of the body. The mind is part of the invisible world of thought, feeling, attitude, and imagination.

To understand this better, let's try a little experiment.

Using your right index finger, point to your brain.

Now, using the same finger, point to your mind.

Not so easy, right?

One way to put it is the brain is the physical aspect of the mind, but the mind is not confined to the brain. For simplicity's sake, for the rest of the chapter, I will use the word "mind" even when referring to the brain, just so it's easier to understand.

The mind has two main parts: the conscious mind and the subconscious mind. The conscious mind is responsible for logic, reasoning, decision-making, and all actions that are performed actively, while you are conscious. For example, if you pick up your coffee cup and take a sip or make a decision to go for a movie later this evening, those were functions of your conscious mind. The subconscious mind is responsible for keeping things stable inside your body, maintaining balance, and maintaining your habits and bodily functions. The fact that you are able to breathe and your heart is able to beat without you constantly having to make it happen is because your subconscious mind is at work. One significant and powerful feature of your subconscious mind that we will dive into in this chapter is that it is a giant memory bank that stores all your life's memories, your skills, your habits, and your beliefs (which you may not even be aware of) and is responsible for the thing called autopilot.

What's an autopilot? More on that in a second. Right now, let's look at this charming little parable first.

Two Fish and the Water

There are these two young fish swimming along, and they happen to meet an older fish swimming the other way who nods at them and says, "Morning, boys. How's the water?"

The two young fish swim on for a bit, and then eventually one of them looks over at the other and says, "What the heck is water?"

This simple story told by David Foster Wallace in a commencement speech is not only endearing but also profound. This story points to a very important idea that the most common realities that we are often used to out of habit and familiarity are often the ones that are the hardest to see.

Let's look at another example that has the same idea but may be more relatable:

In your house, you accidentally bump into a wall with a piece of furniture and scrape off some paint, roughly the size of a coin. You are disappointed and decide to repair it as soon as you can. Then some time goes by and because you are busy, you don't get around to fixing it. And then some more time goes by before something interesting happens-you don't even see that scrape on the wall anymore. It's right in front of your eyes, but out of habit, you've learned to ignore and not *see* it. It's like your mind has created a blind spot for you.

The important idea that runs in both instances is that sometimes certain ideas are so deeply ingrained in our minds due to habit or familiarity that our minds create a proverbial blind spot around them, and we don't even *see* them and therefore don't think of questioning them, just like the fish cannot see water even though they are completely immersed in it.

Similarly, there are many realities in your life that you simply cannot *see* because you are in living *in them.* One such reality is that, just like most people, you have been living your life in an autopilot state. You think you have been flying your plane, i.e. you have been controlling your life, but in reality, it's largely been on autopilot, also known as your subconscious mind. The destination, the altitude, the mechanics, the whole thing has been pre-programmed by your past experiences, societal conditioning, and your beliefs. Most things, if not all, that you have aspired toward in the past or want for the future are learned behaviors; they have been programmed into you from your surroundings.

Yes, you are officially the pilot, but the auto-pilot programming is what's actually flying the plane. If this concept is new to you, then it might sound very abstract and confusing right now, just like the younger fish didn't understand what water was, but bear with me. It will start to make sense soon.

Subconscious Mind: Your Autopilot

Think of your mind as a computer. Just like a computer runs on programming, your subconscious mind, too, runs on its own programming. Broadly speaking, the programming is a bundle of your memories, thoughts, beliefs, skills, and habits. For instance, when you learn to drive a car, it's a very conscious effort initially, but after a few months, the patterns become so embedded in your mind that the whole action of driving becomes subconscious, and from that point on, you drive the car pretty much in autopilot mode.

The subconscious mind's patterns, like skills and habits, are always running in "autopilot" mode. You don't need to overthink or be consciously aware when you are brushing your teeth, using the computer, or putting on your shoes. Any thought, memory, or action that gets repeated or is considered important by your mind becomes a part of your subconscious mind's programming. This is great information to know because this is how habits are formed and skills are acquired, something that we will discuss further in later chapters. For now, let's talk about beliefs and belief systems because they have a significant impact on your life.

So, what is a belief?

A belief is simply an idea that your mind considers to be true.

How does a belief form?

A belief is formed through repetition and/or emotional intensity.

For a belief to have formed, a thought or an idea was either repeated often enough, or it was accompanied with a lot of emotional intensity in your life from credible sources, like parents, teachers, friends, the media, books, or personal experiences until a point came when your mind accepted it to be the truth. For example, if as a child you sang often and were praised by your family and friends, you started to believe "I sing well," or on the flip side, you received a C minus on a math test in third grade, and you were embarrassed to share that with your parents, so you started to believe "I'm not good at math." Once a person accepts a belief as a truth, it becomes a part of the "autopilot" mode.

So why are we talking about beliefs?

Because beliefs drive behavior, and we don't even realize it!

Once you form a certain belief, for instance, "I'm not good at numbers," this belief will become a part of your subconscious autopilot process. Let's explore how it could play out in your life using the example used earlier.

If you believe, "I'm not good at math," you won't even try to become good at it,

and because you don't even try,

you won't get better, and as a result,

you continue to be that person who is "not good at math."

This becomes a *negative* spiral. And in a way, it becomes a self-fulfilling prophecy.

Now let's look at the same situation by replacing the negative belief with a positive one. A positive belief will sound something like this:

"I'm not good at math right now, but I'm willing to learn and get better at it."

So, you will try the math problems, even if it means you might fail at first.

When you fail, *instead* of letting another negative belief like

"See! I know I'm not good at math, so I should stop trying" stop you,

you continue to try harder. You might get a friend to help explain the concepts to you.

As a result,

the more you try,

the better you get with effort and persistence,

which leads to you eventually becoming "good at math." So, it becomes a *positive* spiral.

Now let's look at some other examples of subconscious negative beliefs that would have a significant limiting impact on an individual's life:

- Good things never happen to me.
- I cannot trust anyone.
- Life is hard.
- It's tough to make money.
- I am not a disciplined person.
- I am always taken advantage of.

If a person has all these negative beliefs running on autopilot in their subconscious, it is not a surprise that this person would have a pessimistic outlook towards life and would be far less likely to take risks, take on new challenges, and grow and become better. Therefore, all these beliefs end up becoming up self-fulfilling prophecies.

As the saying goes, *"What you think about, you bring about."*

We all have negative beliefs like these in our life. They are called limiting beliefs because they limit our perception of what's possible, which ultimately limits our growth. One such limiting belief that I had about myself was "I'm not a morning person." I share this story in a later chapter in this book, so I won't go too deep here, but the point here is this: because I considered this to be the truth, I didn't even try to become a morning person. It was not until a few years ago when I made a lot of lifestyle changes that I challenged my limiting belief and forced myself to develop the habit of waking up early. Fast forward to now. Mornings are the favorite part of my day, and I thoroughly enjoy my morning routine.

So, the bottom line is this: what you believe may or may not be the reality, but it *is* a reality in your mind. And one of the biggest predictors of your success in any endeavor is your beliefs. Your positive beliefs will positively impact your chances of success, and vice versa, your negative beliefs will negatively affect your chances of success. Therefore, in order to succeed, it's imperative that you pay close attention to your thoughts, especially the limiting ones, and replace them with positive and empowering ones.

The biggest piece that I want you to take away from this is that your mind holds an infinite number of beliefs. A lot of those beliefs could be limiting beliefs or negative. Those limiting beliefs are sabotaging your chances for growth and success. For example, if you believe "money is evil" on a subconscious level, then it will be very difficult for you to grow financially. Or, if you believe "I'm not a people person," then it will be virtually impossible for you to be very successful in any kind of sales or leadership role because those roles require you to have people skills and high emotional intelligence. So, it's of utmost importance that you pay attention to your thoughts and scan for negative beliefs and challenge them and replace them with positive and empowering beliefs. This is imperative for your personal growth, which inevitably translates to growth in the external world. Find phrases that make you feel inadequate like "This project is a nightmare; how will I ever get through this?" and replace them with empowering ones like "I will figure out a way to execute this project successfully."

Your mind has used all the beliefs you've accumulated in your life, positive or negative, empowering or limiting, to create a "growth mindset" or a "fixed mindset." And because a growth mindset fuels success and is an accumulation of positive beliefs, it would be worthwhile to look at the negative and limiting beliefs and replace them with positive ones.

Garbage Idea #3: Successful People are Lucky

Another "Garbage Idea" that I carried around for most of my life was that successful people are successful because they are *lucky*. Somehow, they were lucky to be at the right place and the right time. Or they were lucky enough to have the right connections. Or they were born into the right family. Or they were just lucky to be born talented or taught by the best.

I'm not sure when exactly this shift happened for me, but I do remember challenging this notion one day and thinking there has to be more to success than just sheer luck (that includes innate talent or smarts). I probed further and asked:

"What are all the world's highest achievers doing differently than what I'm not doing?"

I wondered: what makes someone an outstanding athlete? Or a great leader? Or an amazing parent? Why do some people accomplish their goals while others fail? What makes the difference?

What I learned, or maybe I should say *un*-learned, is that while luck can play an important part in the success of some people, broadly speaking, it is still only a *part*, not the sole reason, for success.

Success is actually a science. A predictable science.

Anyone willing to learn and act on this science can be successful.

The analogy I like to use to make my point about success is it is similar to climbing a mountain. In order to set yourself up for success, i.e. reach the peak, you will need to learn about the mountain-things like the size and height of the mountain, what the terrain is like, the climate, etc. If you are willing to put in the work of:

- Acquiring enough knowledge about the mountain
- Arming yourself with all necessary gear and tools you'll need for the climb
- Preparing yourself physically and mentally

Then, you can climb any mountain you choose.

Now my intention is not to oversimplify the idea; depending on the size of the mountain, there could be some serious work involved. But I really believe that anyone who is truly willing to follow the formula and put in the work *can* climb any mountain they want. It's the same thing with success. There are some common traits that all successful people have. And the great news is, these traits can be learned and developed.

Before we get into the science of success, I do want to make a special mention. Success means different things to different people. For some, success might be financial growth and achievement. For others, it might mean recognition or fame, being acknowledged, or being recognized. For a sportsperson, it might mean trophies. For a parent, it might mean raising great kids that he or she is proud of. For some, being successful might simply mean living a life filled with happiness or purpose.

So, before we go any further, I'd like to mention that I will be using the word "successful" or "successful people" quite often in the book. By doing so, I am *not* referring to a special class of people who have a certain socio-economic status or a certain amount of fame. When I use the term "successful people" or "high achievers" I'm referring to people who have accomplished their aim or purpose that they set out to achieve, whatever that might have been. These people are high achievers in their field of interest. Whatever it means to you, know that the success you desire is more achievable than you think.

So, what are these common success traits? Let's dive in.

Success Trait Number One: Clear Vision

> *"A lack of clarity could put the brakes on any journey to success."*
> – Steve Maraboli

When you get into your car and drive, you know exactly where you want to go. You don't drive around aimlessly and hope to reach a destination that you haven't properly defined, right? That wouldn't make any sense. However, ask most people what they want in life (the destination). Chances are they are not very clear. They think they know what they want; however, their answers are often vague or abstract.

For example, they might say they want to "make more money," or "be successful," or "to grow," or "be happy." You want to be successful? What does success look like for you? What needs to happen for you to feel successful? You want to make more money? How much more? Is it $1K, $10K, $10M? You want to be happy? What makes you happy? You want to grow? Is it career growth, financial growth, or personal growth? You get the point.

In order for you to be able to work towards a goal and a way of life, you must define, with specificity and exactness, what that looks like. Clarity is critical to success. If you don't know exactly what you want, how can you get it? Successful people have a definite sense of direction. They have a clear understanding of what success means to them. Everything they do is consistent with their goals. They look forward and decide where they want to be. Their day-to-day actions help them move closer to their vision.

Gaining clarity must be the number-one priority for anyone seeking success at anything. The first step is to define exactly what it is that you want to achieve. Then, the second step is to break down what is required to get there into many smaller goals. The "how" to break down big goals into smaller ones we'll dive into later in the book, but for now, just know that clarity is power because it significantly increases your chances of achieving your goals.

And then there is the second and most critical component to the element of clarity. It's the biggest driving force behind the success of any goal, and that is to *know your why*. Why do you even want what you want? Why is knowing your *why* so important?

Let's explore.

Why, Oh Why?

> *"He who has a why can endure any how."*
> – Frederick Nietzsche

I had failed often in my life.

In the past, I had signed up for gym memberships and failed to follow through. I'd vowed to:

eat healthier,

read more books,

wake up early,

stop procrastinating,

etc., etc., etc.

The list is a mile long.

And even with the best of intentions, the bottom line was I had not followed through.

Yet in the recent past, I was able to create such a massive and lasting change in my career in such a short span of time. How come? How was I able to make that happen? What was really different this time?

As I looked back at my life and tried to dig deep for the reason, it finally hit me! This time I was very clear on "Why" I needed to make the change, and I had a deep and emotional connection to that "Why."

My family was my "Why." I needed to make the change for my family's future. It was an "either swim or sink" situation, and sinking was *not* an option. I didn't give myself a choice.

I realized the huge impact that seemingly small factor had.

It's often difficult to follow through on things, especially if they are difficult, unless we have a strong enough and compelling reason for the action. As simple as it may sound, your "Why" will be the biggest driving force behind any goal you set for yourself. Be crystal clear on *why* you are doing something, and your chances of accomplishing the goal increase significantly.

Most people don't know *why* they're doing what they're doing. They imitate others, go with the flow, and follow paths without making their own. They spend decades in pursuit of something that someone convinced them they should want without realizing that it won't bring them lasting happiness.

You need to be clear on why you're doing what you're doing. Why is your goal important to you? When your reason for doing what you must do is strong, then if you hit roadblocks when things go wrong, as they always do, you have the strength and purpose to keep going. When you define your dreams and goals with exactness and clarity, you can build the game plan to achieve them and know exactly what you need to do. And knowing your *why* will give you the boost you'll need when going through the rough patches. It will provide the compelling vision that you want to work towards.

Success Trait Number Two: Mental Toughness

There is extensive research backing up the fact that your mental toughness plays a more important role than anything else for achieving your goals in your career, business, health, and life. That's good news because you can't do much about the genes you were born with, but you can do a *lot* to develop mental toughness. I like the term mental toughness because it is a formidable blend of grit, willpower, resilience, and the ability to delay gratification.

Grit

Angela Duckworth, a researcher at the University of Pennsylvania, has shown through her landmark research that grit is a strong predictor of success and ability to reach one's goals. Grit is the perseverance and passion to achieve long-term goals. Angela has found that grit is the hallmark of high achievers in every domain. She's also found scientific evidence that grit can grow. Another way to put it is that grit is one's willingness to be uncomfortable in pursuit of their goals or to improve their current circumstances. It is simply one's ability not to chase comfort but to stay focused on the top of the mountain and be willing to incur the occasional discomfort that comes with the ascent.

Teddy Roosevelt sums up the importance of overcoming fear and managing vulnerability in this brilliant quote:

It is not the critic who counts; not the man who points out how the strong man stumbles, or where the doer of deeds could have done better. The credit belongs to the man who is actually in the arena, whose face is marred by dust and sweat and blood; who strives valiantly; who errs, who comes again and again because there is no effort without error and shortcoming; but who does actually strive to do the deeds; who knows great enthusiasms, the great devotions; who spends himself in a worthy cause; who at the best knows in the end the triumph of high achievement, and who at the worst, if he fails, at least fails while daring greatly.

Grit is about what goes through your head when you fall down and how that-not talent or luck-makes all the difference.

The Stanford Marshmallow Experiment

In the 1960s, a Stanford professor named Walter Mischel conducted a series of well-known experiments known as The Stanford Marshmallow Experiment. During his experiments, Mischel and his team tested hundreds of children-most of them around the ages of four and five years old-and revealed what is now believed to be one of the most important characteristics for success in health, work, and life. Let's talk about what happened and, more importantly, how you can use it.

The set-up of the experiment was simple. The child was presented with a choice:

- have one marshmallow now or
- have two marshmallows in fifteen minutes' time.

The experimenter left the room and would come back in fifteen minutes to see the choice the child made.

The video of the children waiting alone in the room was rather amusing. Some kids simply couldn't wait and jumped and ate the marshmallow as soon as the researcher closed the door. Others held on a bit longer but eventually gave in to the urge a few minutes later. Only a small portion of the children managed to not give in to the temptation and were able to wait the entire time.

As the years rolled on and the children grew up, the researchers conducted follow up studies and tracked each child's progress in a number of areas. What they found was quite amazing. The children who were willing to delay gratification and waited to receive the second marshmallow ended up having higher SAT scores, lower levels of substance abuse, lower likelihood of obesity, better responses to stress, better social skills as reported by their parents, and generally better scores in a range of other life measures. In other words, this proved that the ability to delay gratification was essential for success in life.

If you look around, you'll see this playing out everywhere:

- If you delay the gratification of browsing social media feeds on your phone and get your workout done, then you'll be fitter and stronger.
- If you delay the gratification of splurging on shopping, then you'll be able to save for your future.
- If you delay the gratification of sleeping in and try to wake up early, then you'll be able to get more done in the day.

… and countless other examples.

Success usually comes down to choosing the pain of discipline over the ease of distraction or inaction. And that's exactly what delayed gratification is all about. In some instances, it's essentially about doing nothing. Yes, you're resisting and fighting an internal battle of willpower, and you're having to just sit there and stare at a metaphorical marshmallow for fifteen minutes.

In other instances, it's doing the same thing over and over and over hundreds, maybe even thousands, of times even when it's boring, monotonous, and hard. People who can delay gratification in one area of life can successfully do so in other areas as well.

Mental toughness is a strong trait of all successful people, and it is one that can be developed systematically with consistent practice. This is something we will discuss further later in the book.

Success Trait Number Three: Invest in Their Most Valuable Asset

> *"Your level of success will seldom exceed your level of personal development because success is something you attract by the person you become."*
> – Jim Rohn

Successful people are very clear on what their most valuable asset is. They repeatedly put in time, effort, and energy into growing that asset. So, what is that most valuable asset?

It's their own self.

They treat themselves as their most valuable asset and are constantly looking to grow it by acquiring more knowledge, learning new and improving current skills, and taking care of their health and wellbeing. Successful people invest in themselves. They don't spend their time, money, or energy on things that aren't meaningful; instead, they focus on growing and evolving.

People learn best from mistakes. However, those mistakes don't need to be their own. This is the reason books can be such a powerful learning tool. You can learn vicariously through other people's experiences. A single book could contain decades' worth of wisdom a person may have acquired through life's trials and tribulations, and reading their book gives you a chance to spend time with these wise people and learn through their experiences.

You might've heard the phrase "leaders are readers." High achievers are voracious readers. This is the reason they are often more intelligent, empathetic, and creative, as it improves brain connectivity and function. Reading can inspire you with stories of great accomplishments. It can boost creativity and provide you new ideas.

On a subconscious level, your thinking starts to adapt, and your standards become higher. You can spend a week reading a book of information that an expert took a lifetime to compile. Do that consistently, and you are growing your own inner capacity at exponential rates.

All successful people have coaches and mentors. High achievers are not afraid to put their ego aside and seek coaching and counseling from others. They are open-minded to different perspectives and are flexible and willing to try different approaches to be able to reach their goals. Successful people get guidance from people who have already been successful at what they want. They know that by doing so, they will get to where they want to be faster, with greater efficiency, and better results.

High achievers also understand that willpower alone does not work when it comes to sustained focus and effort over time. Investing in coaches and mentors increases accountability, that supports growth through continuous improvement and does not allow you to play small. I have personally leveraged the power of coaching and accountability consistently in the past few years; this alone is the biggest reason I've enjoyed more progress in every area of my life, personal and business, in a short few years than I had in decades.

CHAPTER 5:

Knowledge Is Useless (E: Execute)

T he knowledge and the insights you have received so far in this book are *useless*.

Absolutely useless.

Yes, you read that right-not a typo.

They are useless *unless* you put them into action. You can acquire all the knowledge in the world and gain as many insights and tools as you can find under the sun; however, none of them will make any difference in your career or life until you take action on them, i.e. *Execute*.

Execution is critical to success!

> *"Without action, you aren't going anywhere."*
> – Mahatma Gandhi

The air was filled with tension.

Both parties were on edge.

Even though it was just another annual performance review at my boss' office, it felt like I was a lamb that had just accidentally strolled into a lion's den, and things were about to get worse.

This was probably one of the hardest reviews I had experienced in my career. It was not hard because my performance in the past year was bad; on the contrary, my work was very much appreciated.

That was not the problem.

The problem was there was a big gap in expectation of what the next salary raise should be.

Our expectations regarding the appropriate number were poles apart. I wanted to be in a higher income bracket because I felt that it was a fair number for the level of work I was doing. Besides, getting this raise was especially important to me considering the huge financial problems I was faced with at the time. So, I stated the number, feeling confident that it was well-deserved. What I didn't realize was that by doing so, I was about to have a negotiation face-off with Goliath.

After a number of back and forth heated arguments came the fateful statement that left me flabbergasted.

"You know, Vandy. You do a great job. But tomorrow, if we wanted to, we could get another Vandy."

Smack!

It felt like I had been slapped in the face.

My ears began ringing.

It was painful.

I wasn't sure what I could have done to deserve this. This was just a business meeting, right? Then how did it get so personal?

I was shocked.

I somehow managed to find the strength and remained calm in the moment. But later that night, anger washed over me.

I was furious!

I thought to myself, "What a horrible thing to say! I work so hard, and this is what I get in return? It's not OK to talk to people like this!"

I slept angry. Disappointed. Hurt.

After some time, thought, and reflection, when the anger had died down a bit, my soft (but tough cookie) inner voice started talking.

She said,

"Yes, it hurts right now, but is that not true?

"Are you really irreplaceable right now?"

"Yes, you put in a lot of hard work, and your work is great, but is it really that outstanding?"

I was confused and annoyed by those questions. I didn't want to answer them. I just wanted to be consoled and told how I was *right* in being angry, not probed with nasty and irritating questions. I wanted the tough-cookie inner voice to shut up and leave me alone. But it didn't.

It nagged me continuously for a long time, and slowly on the inside, I reluctantly started to realize that even though it was bitter, it was in fact the truth.

Yes, I did great work, but I *was* replaceable. Period.

This was a "fork in the road" kind of a moment. I could either choose to remain angry and resentful and think that I was treated unfairly and wronged. Or get up, dust myself off, and use the pain as fuel to drive me forward. I chose the latter.

I decided to make a significant change, to work tirelessly, and acquire new skills that would make me more valuable and elevate the quality of my work exponentially. I wasn't ready to settle for "great" anymore. I was now shooting for *outstanding*!

This decision was about to take my life to a whole other level. With this tougher resolve, I put in a ton of work until I became irreplaceable. It's the decisions we take in these "fork in the road" kind of moments that define our destiny. Having gone through adversity, your life can never be the same. There can only be two outcomes: you can either become *bitter* or *better*.

I chose better, and I became better.

I told myself, *"I will transform myself and take my work to such an extraordinary level that no one will ever think of talking to me that way again!"*

In hindsight, what felt like an insult in the moment was one of the biggest blessings in disguise. Unbeknownst to me, I was settling for less. Yes, I was producing great work, fulfilling all my responsibilities, but I was still coloring inside the lines. I was ready and looking for opportunities but not really going out there and *creating* them. There are many ways to create opportunities, something that I will share in the upcoming chapters. For now, broadly speaking, I'll say this: by thinking outside the box and taking initiatives, being more curious and asking difficult questions, and focusing on adding value, I got promoted multiple times in the years to follow.

The situation I had to face was extremely unpleasant, but I needed that jolt to realize that I had more to me that needed to come out. I needed to dig deep and find that next level inside and manifest it in real life. I was a good employee, but there was a whole other entrepreneurial side to me that I had not tapped into yet.

Yes, I had to endure a *lot* of pressure in a short amount of time. I was already struggling financially, and now this! But I truly believe it all happened for a reason, and the reason was that I was meant to learn and grow from the experience. I needed to be challenged. And if I had a way to go back and change how things occurred then so they weren't as hard and painful, I wouldn't change a thing.

The reason why I share this story is I want to drive home this very important point. Every significant and lasting change is initiated by a strong *decision*. A decision to "burn your boats."

Burn Your Boats

The concept of "burning boats" is often traced back to the story of Cortés and his expedition to capture a magnificent treasure said to be held at an island. Upon arrival, he made history by ordering his men to burn their boats.

Why did he do that?

Quite simple and *brilliant*, by doing so, he sent a clear message: There was no turning back. They would either win, or they would perish.

Two years later, they succeeded in their conquest.

At its essence, "burning boats" simply means a point of no return, a psychological commitment to crossing a line you can never turn back from. There is no room for hesitation. When you're completely all in, nothing will stand in your way.

So, I ask you to take this moment to *truly decide*. I know you want to make a significant change in your life. You wouldn't have gotten this far in the book if you didn't. And I know that you are capable of making the significant change you desire.

But the question is are you ready to make this decision? Are you willing to put in the work and *do* what it takes? Are you willing to burn your boat? If you want this badly enough. If you really decide and follow through. If you put in the work. Then, I'm here to tell you, you can absolutely create the change you desire!

> *"Your life changes the moment you make a new congruent and committed decision."*
> – Tony Robbins

What Do You Really Want?

As we explored in the previous chapter, clarity is power. Being clear and specific on what you want is the first step towards achieving any goal. So, let's start by getting clear on what you want.

The research is conclusive. Dr. Gail Matthews, a psychology professor at Dominican University in California, did a study on goal setting with 267 participants. She found that you are forty-two percent more likely to achieve your goals just by writing them down. Now that's a high percentage!

It's not just important to write your goals down, but it's also very important to be as specific and detailed as possible.

Picture this scenario: my friend, let's call her Rachel, announces her New Year's resolution on Dec 31st is that in the new year she is going to lose weight. That's it. She's going to do it. Fantastic!

Now, this may sound like she is very clear on what she wants. However, if she ends up losing two pounds by next December, do you think she met her goal? I think it would be safe to say no. That is probably *not* what she had in mind.

A lot of times people are not satisfied with their results; however, what they fail to realize is they never defined what an ideal result looks like. In order to increase her chances of successfully reaching her goal, she needs more clarity. She needs to be clear on a lot of things, but at the very least, she needs to know:

- *How* much weight?
- By *when*?
- *What* are the action steps she'll take?
- (And this may seem like a no brainer question, but) *Why* does she want to lose weight?
- A more clearly thought-out goal would be:

What: Lose 30lbs

When: by June 30th

How: Eating healthier and working out more

Then, further specify what eating healthier and working out more means. For example, eating healthier could mean:

- Eat a salad before every meal for a minimum of five days a week.
- Drink 70oz of water every day.

- It could also mean breaking bad habits and replacing them with good ones like; replace the daily breakfast muffin with a bowl of oatmeal.

And, working out more could mean:

- Go to the gym four times a week-three days cardio and one day strength training.
- Taking the stairs at work every day instead of the elevator.

The more detailed she gets in breaking down that goal into actionable steps, the greater her chances of success will be.

And now, once again, as discussed in the previous chapter, being very clear on why she wants to lose weight is a very important step. For instance, if she wants to lose weight because she wants to have a summer body for the upcoming summer, then chances are that when winter comes, she might gain the weight back. Or similarly, if she wants to lose weight for an upcoming event, for example a friend's wedding, then once again, the "Why" behind it is not a very deep and emotional why; therefore, she might struggle to achieve or keep the results in the long run. However, if she really thinks deeply about her "Why" and realizes that the real reason she wants to lose weight is to have more energy at work and home and to do the things she wants to do like make energetic presentations at work, be able to meet more high-pressure deadlines with ease, be able to still have the energy to run after her preschool-aged kids when she gets home at the end of the long workday, and in the long-term be able to live a healthy and long life with her family, she will be more driven to achieve her goals of losing weight and keeping it off.

There are only two reasons why people don't achieve their goals:

1. Either they don't start
2. Or they don't finish.

That's it. It's that simple.

And in both cases, the "Why" can be the distinguishing factor between success and failure. A strong "Why" will help light a fire under you to get started. It will also give you the motivation to keep going when things get tough. If your "Why" is powerful, you will not stop until you achieve your goal.

The Perfect Day!!

So, if the "Why" is so important, then it would make sense to be crystal clear on why you want what you want in your life, right?

Now you might say,

"I know what I want and why I want it."

To that, I'll say humor me. Just play along.

When you complete this exercise, you will know why this seemingly small step can give you surprising clarity regarding what you truly value in life. If you'd like to have more clarity on what you really desire and truly value in your life, this exercise is possibly the most simple and insightful exercise I can offer you. I hope you pause and take the time to use this exercise and really think, go on a deeper level, and let your imagination run wild. The answers you get back may surprise you.

Take a blank piece of paper and write out your perfect day exactly as you would most love it to be. Ask yourself:

- What would my perfect day look like?
- Who am I spending time with?
- Where am I traveling?
- Where am I living?
- What am I working on?
- What did I have for my meals?
- What am I talking about?

Go in as much detail as possible from the time you wake up until the time you are ready to hit the hay.

What Were Some of the Activities You Did?

Run, swim, exercise, study, have a massage, garden, dance, write, sing, travel, teach, serve, work, consult, speak, make love, dream, play… This is your day, so go all out. Let yourself go with this exercise. It's an amazing opportunity to think about what you love doing and who you love doing it with.

This exercise will provide the perspective that could easily get buried inside of us in the 24/7 hustle and grind mode we live in.

When I did this exercise for the first time, I realized that for my perfect day, I mostly wanted to spend time doing things I love with the people I love: my family and my friends.

For instance, I saw myself eating delicious, healthy, organic meals with my family. In terms of activities, I saw myself swimming, playing tennis, walking on the beach under the stars with my husband. There was a lot of joy and laughter. At work, I was working with a group of positive, energetic, motivated individuals. My work was purposeful. What I did was making a positive impact in the world.

As simple and cliché as this may sound, what I realized is family, health, a strong sense of purpose, and happiness are what I value most. What I further realized was that yes, money was important, very important, but as a means to the end I was looking for, not as an end in itself. Sometimes in the race to make more and achieve more, we can lose sight of this very simple fact: money is *not* the end goal; it is only a means to another end goal.

Money is valuable only because it allows you to buy something of value, whether it's something tangible or an experience, or a feeling, for example, a sense of security or freedom. And the more clear you are on what that end goal is, the easier it would be to stay motivated towards achieving your goals.

Looking back, it's so easy to connect the dots, but this simple truth was not as apparent to me before. After the exercise, it shifted to the front and center of my mind. I further realized that I could easily do a lot of the activities that I dreamed about in my perfect day *now*! I did not need to wait for a perfect day to do them.

In an interesting way, even though the perfect day was not directly about money for me, it fueled my desire to make more money in a different way. Now, I wanted to make more for the lifestyle I saw in my perfect day. I wanted to be able to afford everything I dreamed of. It replaced the "need to survive" with a "desire to thrive!" Now instead of feeling the *push* to make money, I started to feel a *pull* towards it. It's interesting to note how a slight shift in perspective could create magic in your life.

Build Your Biggest Asset

Let's see if you are beginning to think like a successful person.

What is your highest income-producing asset?

Yes, spot on! It's *you*!

> *"Give me six hours to chop down a tree, and I will spend the first four sharpening the ax."*
> – Abraham Lincoln

Whenever you set out to achieve something, it might come in handy to invest a lot in the "ax" that you're going to be using. In this case, the ax is you. So, if you sharpen your ax, i.e. grow and become better, then your income will grow as well. Most people don't even think about investing in themselves. This creates opportunity for those who do.

Too often, people put time and energy into things that will not increase their value or ever pay them back, or they prefer to spend money on expensive gadgets, clothes, designer handbags, or shoes rather than investing in themselves to *skill up*. As children, we are taught to pinch pennies and save for the future. Eventually, if we're smart, we learn a penny saved is not a penny earned-it's just a penny. Investing in yourself will force you to shift your thinking from a save-first approach to a mindset of production and growth. First:

- Invest in learning the skills you need to advance in your position, business, and industry.
- Invest in your health.
- Invest in your own personal growth and development.
- Invest in your relationships.

There was a point in my career where I remember thinking to myself, "How do I grow from here? Work harder? Longer?" After having tried these approaches, I eventually hit a ceiling for one big reason. No matter how hard or long I worked, there was something that would not change: the number of hours in the day.

The hours continued to be twenty-four; therefore, my output would invariably hit a ceiling. So, I took a different approach. Instead of focusing on the quantity, I decided to focus on the quality of my work. In order to improve the quality, I decided to *skill up*. I prioritized my personal growth and worked towards acquiring the skills that would help me become a better manager and a leader. I was reading books, taking online courses, and attending seminars that would help me improve the skills like communication, mindset, emotional intelligence, increasing productivity, etc., skills that I would need for management and leadership positions, long before I was offered any such position. So, when the time came, I was prepared. The work that I had put in myself enabled me to hit the ground running when I was offered the opportunity to lead.

At any given point in time, mentally, I'm preparing for the next level by skilling up. I try to preempt the skills I would need at the next level and work towards building them now. This approach has always been invaluable in giving me a much-needed head start on anything I wish to achieve.

Not-So-Good Mornings

As a working mom, I'd often find my mornings to be quite stressful. By the time the alarm would go off, I'd get out of bed groggy, then wake the kids up, nag them to get ready for school on time, pack their lunches, and finally see them out the door.

My entire morning was shot. I felt flustered and behind the eight ball. There was no time left to do anything else except get ready and run to work. And then the same cycle would repeat the next day. So, I'd often promise myself, *"Starting tomorrow, I'm going to start waking up early,"* and with the extra hours I'd get, *"I'll tackle the day like a superhero"* and get so much more done.

Fantastic plan!

Only one problem-waking up early wasn't my thing.

I didn't consider myself a "morning person." I loved to sleep in. So, when the alarm went off, I was anything but ready. The bed was warm and the snooze button-ahh, so close! No change.

And then, to add insult to injury, every time I didn't follow through, I'd beat myself up for lacking the will-power and discipline to wake up early. This went on and on for as long as I can remember until I stumbled upon a life-changing insight. I discovered the superpower of high achievers. There was hope!

Secret Superpower of High Achievers

Chances are that you know someone who is a high performer, who is able to accomplish more in a day than others accomplish in a week. But it's hard to quite put your finger on why this person is so successful. You were either taught or came to believe that such people have a tremendous amount of willpower and are considerably more disciplined than others.

That's a lie!

The truth is high performing people are just ordinary people with extraordinary habits. This might come as a surprise, but in the long run, willpower is *not* the answer to achieving great results; neither is discipline.

It is *good habits*.

Habits are the secret superpower that helps high performers get so much more done in a day. Their day is a bundle of good habits. No matter how much you know or how smart you are, it comes down to what you actually *do*. And there are two ways to do things:

- **First way**: Be very active and conscious while doing it. For instance, first learning how to drive. You have to be very alert and be in a learning mode. Doing so requires focus, attention, and willpower.
- **Second way**: Do things semi-consciously or, as we learned previously, in an "autopilot" state. This is when the task at hand, or behavior, has become a habit through repetition. For instance, once you know how to drive a car, you can do it with little

mental effort. This way of doing things is much easier and automatic.

Over time, it's your habits that will ultimately determine your success.

Let's consider what habits actually are. Habits are simply learned behaviors. Just as you learned to ride a bike or drive a car, you can learn to create new habits that have a positive effect on your work, life, and ultimately success. If you repeat an action enough times, it becomes a habit. Research done at the University of London in 2009 shows that it takes on average sixty-six days for a habit to form.

> *"Motivation is what gets you started.*
> *Habit is what keeps you going."*
> – Jim Rohn

Willpower: The Starter Fluid

So, does willpower not play any role in all of this? The answer: it does but only a small part.

It's like that of starter liquid that's needed to start a fire with logs of wood. In the beginning, when you are trying to form a habit, every day might be a struggle, so you'll need willpower to keep you going. However, if you are able to push yourself consistently for around sixty-six days, then the habit is formed. The habit will run itself. You will not need to exert any extra effort.

Going back to my story of "not-so-good-mornings," when I learned that in order for any habit to form I needed to continuously repeat the activity for a minimum of sixty-six days, I put that theory into action. I pushed myself to wake up early every single morning for a good two to three months.

The first month was hard-the first week was the hardest! There were so many times the voice in my head tried to negotiate with me. Sometimes, the voice sounded like a bully; it was loud and dominating, and it would say,

"This is a dumb idea. You're not a morning person. It will never work!"

And other times, it would sound like a caring friend and try to manipulate me with reason.

"You've been working so hard. You deserve to sleep in. Sleeping in one day is not the end of the world," etc., etc., etc.

Thankfully, I didn't listen to it. I stayed the course like a robot. But then as more and more time went by, magic started to happen. It became easier and easier to wake up early. Eventually, I was able to transform myself from not being a "morning person" to someone who now *loves* her mornings! I used my willpower to slog through *just* long enough until I formed a habit of waking up early. And now, mornings are my favorite part of my day.

I wake up nice and early, often before the sun is up, before my kids are up, and before my husband is up. I get to have some *me* time each and every day because of this habit. I manage to get my workouts in, read, meditate, and journal, along with taking care of my usual mommy chores. It's as if my morning routine has given me a secret superpower that enabled me to get *so* much more done every day, all while helping me create time for my happiness and wellbeing.

> *"We can use decision-making to choose the habits*
> *we want to form, use willpower to get the habit*
> *started, then-and this is the best part-we can allow*
> *the extraordinary power of habit to take over.*
> *At that point, we're free from the need to decide*
> *and the need to use willpower."*
> – Gretchen Rubin

Better Habits for Better Business

As counterintuitive as this may sound, my daily habits help me stack the deck in my favor professionally.

Repetition leads to habits.

Habits lead to routines.

And routines have the power to change your life.

A daily habit routine is especially powerful because it puts you in the right frame of mind to gain the most out of your day, whether it's in terms of something tangible like productivity or in terms of levels of happiness and sense of fulfillment. High achievers know this and therefore have some kind of daily routine in place.

I heard this saying once, and it stuck with me:

"It's not what you do. It's what you do *daily* that makes the difference."

This is the reason I created a daily routine for myself that includes activities that are meaningful to me. In order to become a better version of myself, I consciously try to better myself in three distinct categories:

Mind,

Body,

and Spirit.

And all of my daily goals help me with that objective. My daily routine includes the following activities:

- Read
- Write
- Sweat (exercise)
- Hydrate (drink water; half my body weight in ounces)
- Meditate
- Laugh

- Express gratitude
- Eat colors (fruits and vegetables)
- Plan
- Visualize (my goals)

Let me share an example of how having these personal habits in place helps me show up as a stronger asset at work and enables me to take care of business better. A big part of what I do at work is solve problems. These problems could be people problems, operational problems, or something unforeseen or outside of my or my team's control. Regardless of what the problem is, if I asked you what is the one thing that almost always accompanies a problem, what would you say? If you said any of the following:

- panic,
- worry, or
- emotional overreaction of some kind (anger, frustration, resignation)

you would be absolutely right.

Solving problems can be a difficult task to begin with, but if the people involved fail to manage their emotions in the process, then the problem at hand can multiply and lead to bigger emotional problems, and then, the situation could spiral out of control very quickly.

When emotions go up, intelligence goes down. Evidence of this in the workplace could include the exchange of emotionally fueled emails or inappropriate comments made in anger or many side meetings laced with office gossip, the effect of which could be felt for days to follow. Each one of these is toxic for morale and overall productivity. Therefore, my primary emphasis when faced with any issue is to solve it as quickly as possible so the problem does not multiply into a people or emotional problem.

In order to do so, first and foremost, I have to maintain my focus on the most fundamental step to problem-solving: Stay *calm*.

Panic is contagious.

But you know what else is contagious?

Calm.

By consciously staying calm in a pressure-filled situation, I can not only problem-solve effectively and quickly but also help spread that sense of calm to others around me.

This is where my daily habit routine comes in handy. By taking the time to include activities like working out, reading, watching something motivational, spending time in silence, journaling, etc., I'm proactively taking care of my emotional state and brain function. These things help me maintain a positive and empowered state.

Let's look at exercise, for instance. When people work out, the brain gets more oxygen, and it releases a combination of "good hormones" that help reduce stress, improve focus, concentration, creativity, and overall mood. So, exercise, in a sense, should be considered a no-brainer (pun intended)!

Meditation and journaling have similar benefits.

Each of the activities I have in my daily routine has tangible physiological and psychological benefits. This routine helps me not only handle stress better but also helps me make better decisions and become more productive. This is how better personal habits help me take care of business better.

CHAPTER 6:

Step on the Gas
(A: Accelerate)

How do you move a car forward?

Release the brakes and press the accelerator.

Pretty simple.

In order to build momentum and accelerate your progress, the same thing needs to happen here. Release the brakes: learn about the hidden obstacles that can slow down your progress and get ready to overcome them. Step on the gas: go heavy on the things that promote progress and ride the momentum.

In this chapter we will discuss the three "Accelerators" of success:

- Time importance
- Focus
- Proximity is power

And the three "Brakes" to your progress:

- Negativity
- Self-doubt
- Procrastination and overwhelm

Accelerator #1: Your Most Precious Resource

What is the one thing you can spend all you want but never be able to earn?

If you answered time, kudos to you!

Time is finite. There are only 1,440 minutes in a day-no more, no less. Once you spend time, you can never get it back. This is why time is your most precious resource.

It sometimes takes people a lifetime to come to this profound realization. They say controlling or managing time well increases your productivity. This, in my opinion, is the biggest fallacy. Time cannot be controlled. No matter how hard you try, you cannot stop the clock from ticking or add minutes to your day.

What *can* be controlled, however, are your actions against the time you have. It's what you choose to spend time on.

Most people don't understand how important time is. Picture this: some people would happily stand in line for over an hour if they were promised a free slice of pizza at a local pizzeria opening event. They might think they are getting a "free" slice; however, let's do some quick math here. If the cost of the slice is five dollars and they stood in the line for one hour, then they have valued their time at five dollars per hour! The "free" slice wasn't really free after all.

It is very important to realize that time is invaluable. No amount of money can get it back. This is precisely the reason I called this section "Time Importance", not the usual time management. Spending time mindfully should be treated as a top priority for anyone looking to achieve big goals or simply to have a meaningful and intentional life.

I Simply Don't Have Time

Every day, people say, "I don't have time" when chances are what's actually happening is they don't know where they are spending it. This happened to me years ago (long before I actively build daily good habits or created daily *me* time for myself).

One day, after having complained about the same problem, "I don't have time," for the gazillionth time, I had an aha moment while sitting on a couch watching TV.

My "soft-but-tough-cookie-inner-voice" (yes, that same one that I mentioned earlier … sigh!) said,

"You say you don't have any time, yes?"

I couldn't deny it, so it continued,

"Yet here you are, sitting and watching TV-something you could do for hours on end while the other important things that you've been wanting to do continue to be on the back burner. Just some food for thought."

Aha!

I realized that the voice was right. I had desperately been wanting to fit in more important activities into my day, things that would help me build new skills and grow personally and professionally like reading books, watching insightful podcasts and TED Talks, journaling, practicing mindfulness, or working out regularly to name a few. But I kept running into the same mental dead-end of not having enough time. So, this became another fork-in-the-road moment where I had to decide:

TV or personal growth?

I, very reluctantly, chose the latter.

I gave up watching TV.

This change was hard because I loved watching TV. However, it opened up hours in my day. By giving up one thing, I was able to fit so many more things in my day. This seemingly small change compounded my growth as a person. The more time I spent on acquiring skills, working out, taking care of my health, the more I was able to deliver professionally. For instance, using the time otherwise spent on TV to read books on say, communication, allowed me to improve my communication at work. I was able to not only improve my own communication skills but also help solve and avoid many problems caused due to poor or a lack of communication in general. So, in that sense, the simple (not easy) decision to not spend time on watching TV but using it to learn and grow more paid me back in dividends and continues to do so.

Now, I don't know if this option is palatable to you or not. And I'm certainly not here to tell you that you need to stop watching TV. I simply want to make this point. If you too have a list of things that you wish to get to that will improve your life personally or professionally but struggle to do because you can't find time, then it's important to realize this: you will never "find" time; you'll have to "create" it.

If you wish to create time, all you need to do is this. Make a list of things you spend time on currently; take the time to reflect on the past few days and literally jot down the things you've spent time on. If you want to get really clear and specific, then consider keeping a journal for a few days where you make detailed entries including the exact time spent on each activity. And then make a list of things you wish to spend time on. These may be things that you think you need to do to help you grow as a person-for instance, taking an online class to build a certain skill, working out, reading books, etc. Or these may be things that you want to do because doing them makes you happy and enriches your life like spending quality time with friends and family or "me time," gardening, or spending time in nature. Then, compare the two and start crossing off things that need to go in order to make room for the things that you think are more important in the long run.

After taking the time to analyze and reflect, it will soon become apparent that you have pockets of time that are wasted daily on activities that will not reward you in the long run-let's call them "time-sucks." It could be checking social media feeds for hours, watching TV, or mindless internet browsing to name a few. Find "time sucks" and minimize or eliminate them as much as possible in order to "create" time for activities that are more important in the long run. Set specific priorities. Take things that may be important to you but are not urgent-for example, that concert that you've been wanting to attend, that trip you wanted to take, that Broadway show you wanted to watch-and schedule them in.

Time is the most precious resource we have. There is nothing more valuable than time invested wisely and intentionally. You can use your time as an investment and get anything you want. You can use it to make more money, grow your value by building skills, improving and strengthening your relationships, or taking care of your health. So, it's what you do with your time that really matters. If you can truly learn to see the value of your time, you'll see that with enough time, effort, and persistence, anything can be accomplished.

Accelerator #2: Keep your eyes on the ball

Today, with the intention to drive success and enhance productivity, there is a lot of emphasis on technological tools, with apps and programs designed to save time, manage projects better, improve communication, etc. (all useful in their own way); however, little attention is paid to an incredibly powerful tool that everyone possesses, that has the power to boost performance drastically. That tool is the power of Focus.

The world today is filled with so much noise and distractions. This makes Focus one of the biggest accelerators to the success of any goal. If you are able to drown out the distractions and stay focused on a goal, it not only increases your chances of achieving success exponentially but also gives you an enviable edge over your competition.

Before we get into how we can leverage the power of focus, let's first take a moment to understand what focus is.

Fundamentally speaking, focus is the ability to pay attention to one option. Or as Gary Keller would say, "The *one* Thing." In his amazingly insightful book by the same name, "The *one* Thing," he drives home this simple but profound truth that focus is about identifying the priority, the *one* thing that is the most important thing and staying focused on it until it is achieved.

If you really strip Focus down to its essence, it simply has two parts:

- Say yes to the important things
- Say no to the un-important things

For example, to finish a project, you need to focus and chip away at all the micro-tasks that will help you reach the end goal as well as simultaneously avoid typical distractions such as emails, the urge to snack continuously, or the urge to engage in any small talk with people around you.

So, if it was that simple to focus, then why is it that people still struggle to focus? Is it due to lack of willpower or the plethora of distractions? No, the answer is: focus has more to do with priority than willpower.

Priority and Focus

Today, Ashley had planned to read for twenty minutes before going to sleep. She just got ready for bed, and the moment she slips in and gets ready to pick up her book, her phone dings.

Someone just texted.

She's curious, so she picks up her phone to check the text. It's her friend Julia reminding her of their dinner plans for tomorrow. Ashley smiles as she texts back, then briefly goes online to check the restaurant menu.

Then, somehow makes her way to her social media feed. When she realizes that she'd been distracted, she looks at the clock. She'd been on her phone for over an hour!

How did that happen?

Now it's too late to read, so she decides to sleep.

Now let's picture another scenario. The next day, Ashley is walking out of a restaurant with her friend, who she'd just met up with for dinner. They are at the crosswalk, when all of a sudden, from out of nowhere, a car comes and hits her friend. Her friend is on the ground unconscious.

Ashley, after being shell shocked for a second or two, immediately grabs her phone, calls 9-1-1, and then right after, tries to do her best to take care of her friend while she waits for the ambulance to arrive.

In the first scenario, Ashley is easily derailed from her goal of reading a book because of one simple distraction: her phone.

She was *not* able to stay focused.

In the second scenario, when her friend is hurt, Ashley manages to stay laser-focused on her goal of calling 9-1-1 and doing her very best to take care of her friend. In this case, it did not matter how many unread text messages she had or what her social media feed said. Why was Ashley so easily distracted in the first case and so laser-focused in the second?

What was the difference?

The answer is *priority*.

Most people don't have trouble with focusing. They have trouble deciding. Lack of focus is a result of lack of clarity and priority. When people are not crystal clear on what they want and why they want it, they will easily lose focus and get distracted. When nothing seems like a priority, then *any* pleasurable distraction will swallow your attention. This is why clearly defined goals with a clear "*why*" are key to maintaining focus.

Focus is About Saying No

Want to know why so many companies can't keep up with Apple?

Because Apple is great about saying no.

Nike CEO, Mark Parker, shared in an interview that shortly after becoming CEO, he talked to Steve Jobs on the phone.

"I asked him, do you have any advice?

To that Jobs said, Nike makes some great products.

However, Nike also makes some crappy stuff.

So just get rid of the crappy stuff and focus on the good stuff."

Parker continued,

"And then I expected a pause and a laugh.

There was a pause.

But there was no laugh."

Quite evidently, Jobs was not joking; he was serious. He followed this very advice himself back in 1998 when he resumed the role of Apple's CEO. When he returned to the company, he shrunk Apple's product line from 350 to ten. This counterintuitive approach is the reason Apple is able to deliver incredibly outstanding products by deliberately narrowing their focus and saying no to good so they can focus on the great. The core idea here is to produce outstanding work by leveraging the power of *no*. Jobs says it best:

"People think focus means saying yes to the thing you've got to focus on. But that's not what it means at all. It means saying no to the hundred other good ideas that there are. You have to pick carefully. I'm actually as proud of the things we haven't done as the things I have done."

The lesson here is that once the priority is well-defined, then focus is essentially about saying no to anything that is not a priority. In order to focus on one thing, you must by default ignore everything else. Focus then becomes the key to productivity and excellence because saying no to every other option allows you to focus on the one important one. In other words, focus is more about saying *no* than it is about saying *yes*.

Set Yourself Up for Success

Focus thrives on proactive planning. Instead of wishing you had more focus when you need it, proactively create an environment that will help you build focus. For instance, if you need to work on an important project in the next few days, instead of relying on your willpower to stay focused and use your energy fighting distractions, set yourself up for success by planning the process in advance:

- Analyze the scope of your project and create a breakdown of the hours you'll need to dedicate to your project each day. Then, assign "focused action time" slots in the day for the entire length of the project.

- For example, it's not enough to think I need to finish the project by Monday next week. Instead, create a plan. It could look something like this:
    - Total project time: fifteen hours
    - Three hours per day times five days
    - Monday through Friday this week
    - 9 a.m. to 12 p.m. every day-"focused action time"

- Switch off or silence notifications on your phone during this time. One casual glance at your phone to check the latest text can easily dilute your focus and waste a significant chunk of your allotted time.

- Find a quiet place or a way to work that can help minimize distractions. For example, when working from home, I almost always wear my noise-canceling headphones. This helps me avoid getting distracted by common household sounds. This seemingly small step goes a long way in helping me stay focused on the task at hand, and I'm able to execute better using less time.

- Give people a heads up that you will be temporarily unavailable during your "focused action time."

The Myth of Multitasking

The modern world is infatuated with the idea of multi-tasking. The myth of multi-tasking is that being busy is synonymous with being productive or efficient.

The exact opposite is true.

You can't be great at one task if you're constantly dividing your time many different ways. Every time you try to multi-task and think that you are doing two or more things simultaneously, you are essentially simply *switching* between tasks. Technically speaking, you are capable of doing two things at the same time. It is possible, for example, to listen to music while driving or talk on the phone while cooking. What is not possible, however, is *actively focusing* or concentrating on two tasks at once. Your brain can only focus on one task at once. If you happen to be successfully performing two tasks at once, then at least one task is on *auto-pilot* mode, something that we explored in the previous chapter on the subconscious mind. However, when you are trying to multitask and do two tasks that require focus, you are actually forcing your brain to switch back and forth very quickly from one task to another. This may *seem* productive, but it's actually quite counter-productive because it puts added pressure on your brain. Multitasking forces you to pay a mental price each time you interrupt one task and jump to another.

As a society, we've allowed ourselves to be seduced with the concept of "being busy." People wear the word "multi-tasking" like a badge of honor; "doing a lot of things simultaneously" is considered a good thing. Quite often, a lot of activity is misunderstood for a lot of results. The underlying thought is, *"I'm always so busy. If I'm doing all this work, I must be doing something important."*

This is a misjudgment.

Focused attention and the ability to monotask leads to better productivity and quality results. Study world-class performers in any field-athletes, artists, scientists-and you'll discover one characteristic runs through all of them: *focus*.

Focus and R.A.S.

If focus was a superhero, then like every superhero it would need a sidekick, and Focus's sidekick would be R.A.S.

What is R.A.S.? Let's explore.

Have you ever noticed that when you buy a new car, you suddenly see that same type of car more often on the road? Or when you learn a new word, you suddenly hear it everywhere. Or how you can hear your name clearly even if you're in a noisy room full of talking people.

What is the reason for that?

The reason is a system that your brain has. It's called the Reticular Activating System. It's a system in the network of neurons that allows certain information in your brain and blocks out other information; it's basically a filter. This filter leaves out the "noise" and helps you focus only on the things that your brain thinks are important or is constantly thinking of.

Why do we have this "filter" or the reticular activating system? There is a really important reason for it, and it is this: if your brain lets everything in, say from a Facebook page, for instance, there is so much information in a single page with the number of photos, ads, words, and buttons, it's information overload. If your brain took in everything at equal value, your head would literally explode off your shoulders. Your brain would melt down. And so, the reticular activating system protects your brain by filtering information and only letting in stuff that it agrees with.

Guess who programmed your filter? You did, based on your past experiences, and so did the people from your past. This filter, as we've learned in the chapter on the subconscious mind, is a part of the "autopilot," the programming of your brain. This filter could have very positive implications or very negative ones. If you think that people at work don't like you, then guess what? Your reticular activating system is going to go through the day and point out every single piece of evidence that confirms the negative belief that you have. So, you get more and more convinced that people at work don't like you.

On the flip side, just like any system, it has its positive side as well. And the positive side is this: if you deliberately take time out of your day to visualize your goals, then you are reprogramming your filter. Now, your brain will start to spot opportunities that will help you get closer to your goals. Your brain starts to spot evidence that things are working out.

It is for this exact reason that I have a vision board in my bedroom. It has a lot of images on it that are meaningful to me and my family. One of them happens to be a book cover. I got the *crazy* idea to write a book over a year ago. I call it crazy because, as I mentioned earlier, I didn't think of myself as a writer and had never even dreamt of becoming one. It just seemed like a very far-fetched thought, something that I could possibly entertain for fun but not actually work towards. Anyway, no matter how much I tried to ignore the idea, it simply did not leave me alone. In fact, it started to nag me. I couldn't shake it off. It nagged me enough to want to create a book cover for it. So, I did. And I put it up on my vision board. Every day since then, it has been in front of my eyes, and guess what? After having stared at it for over a year, it actually materialized. The dream that once seemed "crazy" is now a reality!

I cannot recommend the power of visualization enough. Having a vision board that has pictures of everything you dream of can be a huge accelerator to your success. A picture is worth a thousand words. When you look at a picture, areas of your brain light up that would not respond to language, and your RAS (reticular activation system) gets activated, which means now your subconscious mind is hard at work trying to work towards scanning opportunities that will help you in meeting your goals. So, go ahead and make your goals visual. Put them up in places where you will see them often, use pictures along with written text. This will engage your R.A.S. and now your sub-conscious mind will be working towards helping you achieve them even when you are not actively thinking about them. It's a very powerful tool.

Accelerator #3: You Are the Company You Keep

Your life is going through constant osmosis. This osmosis is a direct result of what you choose to surround yourself with. In the words of Jim Rohn:

> *"You are the average of the five people*
> *you spend the most time with."*

Your life is a direct result of your thoughts. Your thoughts are directly influenced by the company you keep. Therefore, whether you choose to acknowledge it or not, the people you spend the most time with shape who you are. They affect your way of thinking, your self-esteem, and your decisions.

Of course, everyone is their own person, but research has shown that people are more affected by their environment than they realize. It's a fact of life that some people hold us back while others propel us forward. You cannot hang out with negative people and expect to have a positive life. However, on the flip side, if you hang out with people who are better than you at certain things, then that will motivate you to do better as well.

For instance, let's look at the contrast in these two scenarios:

You play tennis with a buddy of yours that is half as good a tennis player as you are. Or you play with another player who is a tennis pro-easily twice as good as you. If you play with the pro consistently for a few games, do you think your game will eventually improve?

Without a doubt, yes.

You will feel pushed to improve your game, to level up, or at least get closer to the pro's level.

I once had the privilege to learn from Frank Shamrock, the MMA legend, author, entrepreneur, and philanthropist. He shared a formula he likes to call *"plus, minus, and equal to"*. He recommends spending equal amounts of our time with:

- People who are better and more successful than you, the "pluses," so that you can learn from them and be inspired.
- People who are equal to you; these could be your

peers or your competition, so that they push you to become better.

- And lastly, the minuses; these are people you can teach and mentor so you can not only add value to their life but also to your own by paying it forward and gaining a sense of purpose in the process.

Tony Robbins says that if you wish to make a significant change in any area of your life then the first thing you should do is "raise your standards." One great way to do so is to constantly keep the company of great people through their work and content and try to model their success by doing what they do. Your physical environment has the ability to empower you or disempower you, so it's very important to be vigilant about what you allow yourself to be exposed to. I personally am a huge fan of interviews and podcasts of high performers. Watching such content on a regular basis not only provides me with strategies, tactics, tips, and tools to improve my performance, but even more importantly, *it elevates the level of my thinking.* Their high standards begin to sound like the new normal. Pushing myself to do better, constantly working on learning and growing, acknowledging fears and moving past them, being comfortable with the uncomfortable, having a big vision, and dreaming big-all these ideas seem like the *obvious* thing to do.

You are continuously becoming the average of the five people you spend most of your time with. So, surround yourself with positive, big thinkers, also known as "battery chargers," as opposed to negative, mediocrity-minded people, also known as "battery drainers."

Proximity Is Power

Jesse was an absolute livewire on stage. His energy and passion were infectious. I first saw him at a big seminar in Vegas where he captivated nearly five thousand people with his insanely funny and bewitching life and business stories.

Jesse Itzler is the author of the New York Times bestseller, *Living with a Seal*, co-founder of Marquis Jet, the world's largest private jet card company later sold to Berkshire Hathaway/NetJets. Jesse also partnered with Zico coconut water and sold it to The Coca-Cola Company. He has also run ultramarathons up to a hundred miles long.

At this seminar, my husband and I had the opportunity to join one of his coaching programs that was a combination of physical challenge, mindset, and business coaching. Joining this program has been one of the best decisions of my life; by becoming a part of this program, I was now spending time with people who were not only extremely successful at business but also were ex-NFL players, ultramarathoners, and Ironman finishers. These people had a strong mindset and a formidable work ethic. In a short span of sixty days, these people managed to inspire me beyond words, and physically, I was pushing myself beyond my perceived limits. I learned so much just from being a part of a crowd of overachievers. Their strong mindset and motivation rubbed off on me and helped me become a better version of myself.

This is the power of proximity.

I cannot recommend it enough. Surround yourself with people who have a strong mindset, big dreams, who think big, play big, who are constantly working on themselves and working towards growing and become better versions of themselves. That attitude is contagious and synergistic; it is bound to rub off and multiply.

"The Brakes"

Now that we've explored how to step on the gas and accelerate, another thing you must check is to make sure that you are not experiencing unnecessary drag due to emergency brakes being activated. That could look something like this.

You set a big goal. You have a plan in place. You feel fairly confident that you can make it happen. And yet, for some weird reason, you freeze in your tracks and don't start. Or start and then feel stuck, unable to move, or dragged down. Or you self-sabotage and give up.

She says she wants to run a 5K but never signs up for it.

He says he wants to get to the next level at work but sabotages that important presentation due to lack of preparation.

She says she wants to launch her business but struggles to start because she buries herself in never-ending research.

He says he wants to sharpen his mind and improve his skill set but never gets around to reading the books on his must-read list.

Why is it so difficult for people to do what they set out to do?

What is that thing that holds them back?

Brakes.

The human mind has built-in brakes. It's the voice in your head that tells you:

"Think about it some more,"

"You're not ready,"

"This thing sounds stupid,"

"Be cautious,"

"Don't do it,"

"Wait for the right time,"

"Who do you think you are,"

"You don't need this."

Brakes are the invisible force that will either freeze you in your tracks, make you incapable of starting, or drag you down as you try to move forward towards the finish line. The brakes are the reason why that business never got launched, the idea that was never explored, the project that got scrapped mid-way, the raise you never got because you never asked for it or the book you didn't write.

Let's look at the three common kinds of "*brakes*" that are bound to show up so you can understand what they look like and how to move past them.

Gatecrasher

What will almost always show up to the party uninvited, when you set a big goal?

An elephant.

Yup.

A big goal or challenge can feel like an elephant. And a fat one at that. So, an important question would be-how do you eat an elephant?

One bite at a time.

There have been times in the past when I've set audacious goals for myself. One, for instance, was the physical challenge that involved doing hundreds of burpees, push-ups, lunges, crunches, sit-ups, etc. in a single routine. I remember being very, very overwhelmed simply by looking at the schedule on certain days.

"How am I going to get through this?" I'd think to myself.

It is at those times when I had to remind myself that I simply cannot gulp the elephant down in one go, no matter how hard I try, so the only thing I could do is to chunk it down into bite-sized pieces (mini-goals) and focus just on the next bite, knowing that by doing so that over and over, I will soon be done with this elephant.

So, in this instance, I'd just focus on the next ten sit-ups, give myself a break and then start again, and when I started again, I only focused on the next ten until I reached the finish line. Sometimes it would take me hours to finish a routine that someone who was in better shape than me would finish in half the time I took. There were times when I'd finish my routine with tears in my eyes. Basically, the journey to the finish line was often tedious and messy, but what's important is that I finished, and I didn't quit. What mattered in that moment was that I continued to put one foot in front of the other. I kept moving forward, no matter how slow.

> *"It does not matter how slowly you go*
> *as long as you do not stop."*
> - Confucius

Some other tips for keeping the elephant in perspective:

Celebrate Your Wins

Each time you reach a milestone, celebrate it! Treat yourself to something you love. Your brain loves rewards. The more you take time to celebrate and reward yourself, the more your brain will register it as a positive memory, something it will want to move towards. For instance, I'm in the first edit phase of my book right now, and a massive amount of resistance is showing up-perfectionism, feelings of overwhelm, self-doubt, you name it. This is exactly why I'm solely focused on taking action, putting one foot in front of the other. And I've also built in a reward for reaching this mini-goal; when I'm done with this first edit in a few days, I'll treating myself to a ninety-minute body massage! Just the sound of it puts a smile on my lips and makes my fingers type faster.

Enlist Helpers

Surround yourself with people who will support you. They may be friends, colleagues, family members, a coach, or a mentor. Keep connected to people who inspire, encourage, and challenge you. Also, practically speaking, enlist people who can help you with any chores that could be time-sucks-for example, cleaning your house, laundry, grocery shopping, walking your dog, etc.-so you can free up your precious time and use it towards working on your goals. By delegating time and energy-consuming chores, you will free up valuable mental space that will help you deal with the overwhelm when it shows up.

Trust the Process

During the journey from the starting line to the finish line, you will have good days, and you'll have bad days. Some days, all your stars will be in perfect alignment, things will run smoothly; you'll have all the motivation you need to crush your goals, and you'll feel unstoppable. And then there will be other days when you'll struggle with finding the drive to keep going. Things will fall apart. You might be bogged down with self-doubt or pessimism. It's inevitable. It happens to everyone-yes, even people who are at the top of their game. What's important to do on those bad days is to remind yourself to keep moving forward.

Ride the momentum

Running is an acquired taste for me. I wasn't naturally inclined to it. It took me time and effort to get used to it. One thing I noticed with it was if I ran a certain number of miles every day consistently, it felt easier to continue, but if I stopped for a few days and then came back to it, it was much harder. So, the lesson in this for me was don't break the chain. Getting the ball rolling is the hardest thing to achieve, so once you have momentum, ride it, step on the gas pedal, and don't take your foot off. The days when you want to skip, remind yourself that it'll be much harder to resume once the streak is broken.

Disappointment Due to Lack of Progress

It's human nature to look for the path of least resistance. We tend to look for that magic bullet, that hack, that secret formula that will fix and make everything all right over-night. And we want it pronto!

When we don't see the results right away, we get disappointed. Well, here's the reality: apart from being improbable and unrealistic, most things just don't work that way. Lasting change takes time, effort, and patience.

This is why I love the story of the Chinese bamboo tree. You take a little seed, plant it, water it, and fertilize it for a whole year, and nothing happens. The second year, you water it and fertilize it, and nothing happens. The third year, you water it and fertilize it, and nothing happens.

How discouraging can this be, right?!

The fifth year, you continue to water and fertilize the seed, and then, something amazing happens! Sometime during the fifth year, the Chinese bamboo tree sprouts and grows *ninety feet in six weeks*!

Wow. That's amazing, isn't it?!

So, did the bamboo tree lie dormant for four years only to grow exponentially in the fifth?

The answer is quite obvious. No.

The little tree was growing underground, developing a root system strong enough to support its potential for outward growth in the fifth year and beyond. Had the tree not developed a strong foundation, it would not have sustained its life as it grew.

Lasting change and sustainable success are much alike to this growing process of the bamboo tree. Progress could be so slow and small in the beginning that it could be very discouraging. You could be taking action consistently, but there is no significant growth to show for it. It is imperative that at this time you remind yourself that if you continue to do the right thing and be persistent, things will happen. And finally, you will begin to receive the rewards.

If you want to acquire new skills that will boost your career or business, lose weight permanently, or if you intend on having successful relationships, you need to plan to work on it for the long haul. For instance, if you want to lose twenty pounds of weight, you cannot do it by eating a healthy and small portion for only one day. Instead, you need to stick to a plan where, in a nutshell, you consume fewer calories than you burn on a daily basis consistently over a given period of time. Then you'll begin to lose weight slowly and steadily.

Likewise, to nurture a great relationship, you can't be affectionate and kind to someone for a day or two and then expect to have an understanding or a connection. It will take days, months, sometimes even years to build a trusting, mutually fulfilling relationship. It cannot happen overnight.

Getting success in business and life is more or less similar to growing a bamboo tree. You have nothing to show for a long time, and the people around you begin to judge you. They urge you to quit. To that, I say as long as you're putting in the work consistently, maintain faith in what you're growing. Other people cannot see what you can see-your bamboo tree is expanding its roots to sustain the impending spectacular growth that is bound to come. You will get those results sooner or later, but you must believe in your bamboo tree and continue to water it.

"Can't Stop Worrying!"

"Mom, I'm so nervous about my French test. I can't stop worrying about it!

What should I do?" My daughter asked as she nervously paced in my bedroom while getting ready for school.

I was slightly surprised that she felt nervous about her French test. "Of all the subjects, French? Really?" I thought to myself.

The reason I was surprised was because she was exceptionally good at it-so good that her French teacher had once jokingly told us that she could be her substitute and teach the class any day. And yet, here she was, feeling nervous, doubting herself despite her remarkable capability.

Then I was soon reminded that this was not a question of ability or preparation; this was a classic case of the human mind becoming its own enemy.

So, I told her, "Pick up your guitar, and sing your favorite song for a few minutes."

She was a bit surprised and almost annoyed to hear this, so she said,

"Mom! That's not going to help me. It's only going to distract me."

"Exactly-that's the point!" I responded excitedly.

This stopped her in her tracks. Now she was staring at me as if I had two heads. I smiled and continued on.

I told her when feeling nervous or worried about a situation, it's best not to fight those feelings but to simply interrupt them by distracting yourself. It's a good idea to shift your focus to something pleasurable like doing something you love. By doing so, you change your thoughts from negative to positive instantly.

She listened quietly and attentively and left for school soon after. A few days later, she shared cheerfully that she got a 100% on her test.

When pursuing anything worthwhile and challenging, know that worries, nervousness, and self-doubt are bound to show up. No matter how high your confidence level and self-esteem is, there will be days when you'll doubt your decisions, your actions, and your abilities. You'll worry about the smallest and most inconsequential details.

"Am I doing this right?" or

"What if I'm wrong?" or

"What if I fail?" or

"I'm so worried" are the kinds of thoughts that are bound to come up. Once again, surprise, surprise! You are not alone. It happens to everyone, even the highest achievers of the world. So, I have a mantra in place for these thoughts: Expect them, don't *accept* them.

On the days when negativity shows up, don't try to fight or suppress it-it won't work. Instead, simply interrupt the pattern by proactively shifting your focus to something fun and pleasurable. Go for a walk, listen to music, read something positive or motivational, play with your kids, pet your dog or cat, or watch something funny. Do something, anything that can snap you out of that negative frame of mind. Even better, have your list ready so you know exactly what to do.

As we've explored in the previous chapters, whenever you are worried or stressed, your body goes into fight-or-flight mode, this shuts down the rational part of your brain. You temporarily lose access to the most advanced part of your brain: the pre-frontal cortex. Not having access to this part can be dangerous because it is this part that helps you make rational and good decisions. Decisions made while you are stressed, i.e. in the survival mode, may not be as sound and well thought out, therefore, they could further escalate the problems, which in turn might give you more to be stressed about, and this could easily become a vicious cycle. Therefore, it's extremely important to break this cycle by doing something that brings you out of survival mode. As simple as this may sound, doing something pleasurable does that. It calms the brain down, and soon, you will regain control of the entire brain instead of just a part of it and now not only do you feel better, you become more efficient and effective at whatever you are applying yourself to. Needless to mention, this would help improve the quality of your results tremendously.

CHAPTER 7:

What Do You Get Paid For? (D: Deliver)

S o far in the book, the focus has been on how to build a solid foundation for success by growing and transforming on a personal level. Now, it's time to take that foundation and build upon it by delivering value to the business world.

Deliver Value

"Try not to become a man of success, but rather try to become a man of value."
– Albert Einstein

Do you know what you get paid for?

For doing your job?

For running your business?

For making sales?

For working hard or smart?

For being efficient and proactive.

The correct answer is none of the above.

None of these answers is correct because they are incomplete. Fundamentally speaking, people, whether they are in a job or running their own business, get paid for one thing and one thing only: delivering value to the marketplace.

People get paid to either help solve a problem or improve other people's lives in some shape or form. Their impact could be big or small, but essentially speaking, they are getting paid to add value to others.

So, if you want more money, add more value. And if you really want to grow exponentially, then get *obsessed* with delivering value. Just having a desire or years of experience doesn't mean that's what the business or your customers need or want.

So how do you add more value to the marketplace?

First step: Add more gas to the fire. Whether it's a job or your own business, do more of what's working for you. However, when I say do more, I don't just mean more; I mean more *strategically*.

What do I mean by that?

At one point in my career, I asked myself a very powerful question, the answer to which became a game-changer for me. Using the 80/20 rule as a foundation, I asked myself: What are the twenty percent of activities that bring me eighty percent of my results?

After some careful reflection, I realized that every time I took some extra time to think deeply and plan ahead, as in, go the extra yard and plot out all details, even preempt potential pitfalls and how to avoid them, it helped me execute projects much easier. This reflection in conjunction with a golden nugget of wisdom I'd gained from one of Arianna Huffington's speeches helped me make a very important shift. Huffington, in her speech, illustrated the difference between a good leader and a great leader. She said a *good* leader is one who does a great job of saving people and minimizing damage when the *"Titanic"* hits an iceberg. However, a *great* leader is one who preempts the icebergs and steers the *Titanic* in advance so that the ship never hits the iceberg and ends up staying safe and afloat.

Once I realized thinking and strategizing were my strengths that brought me the majority of the results I desired, I doubled down on it by consciously spending more time thinking about projects before starting rather than jumping in and trying to figure things out later. By laying a good foundation of a strategic, well-thought-out plan, I ended up helping with the execution significantly. It helped me preempt obstacles or issues in advance and work towards avoiding them in the first place. This was a much smoother approach.

If you happen to be in sales, you can ask yourself the question, which twenty percent of my actions or customers are contributing to eighty percent of my sales? By answering that question, you will identify either the actions that you need to double down on or the customers that you need to focus on to increase sales.

The second step would be to find new ways of adding value. Here are some ways to add value to a business:

1. Increase income
2. Decrease expenses
3. Improve the efficiency of a process
4. Improve the quality of a product or service
5. Solve a problem
6. Prevent a future problem

When considering setting a goal in any of these categories, remember to set meaningful and strategic goals that "move the needle." Whether you plan to add value by increasing income or decreasing expenses, make sure whatever you're looking to do is significant enough to move the needle monetarily or in another way as long as it is quantifiable. Anything less will not make a difference.

When thinking of adding value, don't hesitate to think outside the box. One of the ways my team and I were able to add value to the organization of the company I work for was by cutting back how many samples we produced in China a year. As someone whose responsibility was to create design collections, thinking of adding value by cutting back on samples was a slightly out-of-the-box approach. But this approach alone helped the company save on expenses well into the seven figures in a single year.

Find ways to improve the processes. One of the statements that cost businesses a lot of money is:

"This is how we've always done business."

Never have that mentality. Be curious and question often. Ask yourself,

"Does this continue to make sense?", or,

"if we could start afresh and come up with a new, more efficient and effective process, what would that look like?"

Take the Lead

Everyone has the choice to be a leader, to make an impact. Too many people back off from pursuing this path in the mistaken belief that leadership and greatness are reserved for a select few. But in the many years I've been in business, I have witnessed first-hand that

"The most common way people give away their power is by thinking they don't have any."

Let me repeat.

"The most common way people give away their power is by thinking they don't have any."
– Alice Walker

If you're the kind of person whose foundation is positivity, service, guiding, and supporting others while trying to solve problems and come up with new solutions, you will soon find yourself standing out and setting yourself up to become the kind of leader others respect and want to follow (whether or not you have the title of a leader yet). The title usually follows as well.

Now, you might think, "Easy for you to say. You are already in a leadership position." Let me remind you, it was *not* always this way. I had to work my way up. I remember this one time years ago, long before I was in any kind of leadership position, the company that I worked for had its semi-annual summit. At the summit, the CEO of the company, during his speech, shared an inspirational quote from one of his favorite books and later made an offer. He said if anyone was interested in reading this book, they were welcome to come borrow it from him.

"I wonder if he is serious about the offer?" I thought to myself.

I wasn't sure, but a tiny voice inside me suggested that I take him up on it. So, I walked into his office the next day and asked him,

"Were you serious about the offer to borrow the book? If yes, then I'd like to borrow it." He looked at me briefly, with a slightly puzzled smile, and then offered me the book. I guess I may have been the only person who had taken him up on that offer. I'm still not sure. But I thanked him and started walking out of his office back to my cubicle, hoping he hadn't seen my hand shake as I took the book from him.

The next day, with my heart beating furiously, I walked into his office again with a calm look and a slightly nervous smile on my lips. This time, I had brought along some notes that I had taken during the company summit. I asked him if he had a few minutes to talk about some ideas that had crossed my mind during the recent summit.

He had a hint of curiosity in his eyes as he nodded slightly, suggesting I share.

So, I did.

All while the voice in my head kept on saying, "This is a bad idea. Stop talking! No one wants to listen to these dumb ideas!"

I stood there and shared an example, maybe two.

He listened.

And then, with the serious poker face look that he usually had, he gestured at me to take a seat in front of him.

I sat down.

This was one of my initial steps on a long journey to finding my seat at the table. Here's a gist of how it happened:

One of the thoughts I shared with him was simply this,

"Why does our product development process have to be so crazy every season?

I feel there *has* to be an easier way."

Now, it's important that I make it very clear that I didn't come in with a full-fledged plan on how to solve the problem. All I shared at that point was a gut instinct. It was simply a *feeling* that things could be improved. Listening to and acting on gut instincts like these have been one of the best things I've done for my career and personal growth. By taking this seemingly small step of sharing an abstract idea and initiating a discussion about improving things, I had spurred something important. And now, it was time to go further. I dove deeper and came back with many more concrete plans and strategies to help make the process smoother and more efficient. All of this eventually resulted in a new division being created in the company, and I was asked to head it up.

Speak up.

Share ideas.

Take initiative.

Offer solutions to better things.

Help fix things.

Look for opportunities to add value to conversations. More often than not, your ideas and suggestions might not be implemented, and that's okay! That's just how the process goes. Most ideas don't end up seeing the light of day. It might take a hundred ideas to be rejected before one gets applied, but don't let that discourage you. If you put yourself out there constantly and continuously take initiative with a genuine intention to add value and improve things, then sooner or later, things do start to shift, and people do start to take notice.

First Scratch Their Back, Then They'll Scratch Yours

No matter what kind of business you're in, there is a 100% chance that you have to deal with people.

Business is controlled by people.

And people are controlled by their emotions.

So, if you want to be more effective in your business or your job, gain a better understanding of how to effectively deal with the *emotions* of the people you interact with.

> *"If you want to go fast, go alone.*
> *If you want to go far, go together."*
> – African Proverb

One of the biggest problems that organizations face are people problems. The work itself is not that difficult, but the noise and friction that are created on the way with multiple personalities and egos coming together are what make it difficult. This is why management and leadership positions sit higher on the corporate pyramid. Because the responsibility is bigger, you are not only responsible for your own performance, but also of people and teams that you lead and manage. These positions usually require a more evolved skillset, the ability to handle stress and pressure, and they require a high emotional intelligence.

People are inherently self-centered. I don't say that in a negative way but simply as an acknowledgment of basic human behavior. So, in any interaction, people are usually seeking to serve themselves and solve their problem ahead of yours. Their brain is basically saying, "What's in it for me?"

So, if you want to increase your impact with them, then learn to put their needs ahead of yours. Satisfy their needs first, and then, they will be more receptive to serving your needs.

One of the most common needs that all humans have is the need to be heard, respected, and be cared for. You can form meaningful relationships if you are able to take the time to listen to people's needs, understand where they are coming from, and show them you care. If they feel heard, respected, and cared for, they will be able to trust you, which in turn will significantly improve your working relationship with them. They will be more willing to work with you and even go out of their way to help you if needed. You will have deepened your impact with them, which means the quality of the results produced from this working relationship will also be higher. But this must be done with integrity. People have a built-in bull-crap meter. Sooner or later, if your intentions are not virtuous, they will be able to see through it, and then you will be back to square one or even worse with the issue of lack of trust.

Building relationships authentically takes time. There is a lot of consideration, thought, and effort that goes into it, but they are incredibly rewarding. That's how you can leverage the power of one of the most valuable resources on the planet: human beings.

Leadership and Influence

"Be the change you wish to see in the world."
– Mahatma Gandhi

I did not see the tsunami coming.

But there it was.

I had just been offered the big promotion that I'd worked so hard for. This obviously made me happy but also quite emotional. And then, I'm not sure what was the exact question that he'd asked, but I do remember the moment he asked the question, my demeanor turned from proper to a hot mess in a matter of seconds. My face contorted uncontrollably as I started to sob.

"Where did this come from? What the heck is happening?" the voice in the head asked as I drowned in a sea of overwhelming emotion.

I remember being equal parts insanely embarrassed and yet totally incapable of stopping this ridiculous thing from happening!

I had never been so emotionally vulnerable in a professional setting before. I had always prided myself in being able to manage my emotions well. At work, I barely ever lost my cool, let alone shed tears in a business meeting. But this time was different. The floodgates had opened. I was *not* in control.

Tears just kept flowing out of my eyes.

"Get a hold of yourself. You are not a cry baby!!!" I tried to remind myself over and over to no avail.

To make matters worse, the person sitting across from me was not an average Joe; he was the head of the company I worked for. It was so, *so* embarrassing. This was not me. I've always been proper-then where did this come from?

I kept sobbing and saying nonsensical things while, to my infinite surprise, he sat there handing out tissues and listening compassionately without passing any judgment or jumping to any conclusions. Here was someone who was always so busy and constantly pressed for time, yet he sat there patiently as if he had all the time in the world. My words may have been incoherent, but he was paying close attention. His actions seemed to suggest that everything I shared mattered to him.

As I reflect upon that incident, the over-arching thought that crosses my mind is this: to treat someone in such a vulnerable position with so much dignity and respect is leadership of the highest order. When someone shows you their scars and imperfections, know that a *sacred* space has been created. There is trust in that space. It is important that the sanctity of such a space must never be violated. Great leaders know this.

Leadership is often misunderstood as a skill that requires one to display power, posture, or dominance. Whereas the true essence of leadership can be easily summed up in one word, and that word is: *influence*.

True leadership is the ability to influence others positively, and there is no greater influence than emotional influence. If you are able to move people emotionally in a positive way, you have influence over them.

> *"People will forget what you said,*
> *people will forget what you did, but people*
> *will never forget how you made them feel."*
> - Maya Angelou

People will learn from you, listen to you, respect you when *they* feel respected and understood, not when you're understood. This is the foundation for persuasion and influence. Compassion creates connection, and connection can help you understand the pains, needs, and desired outcomes of those you serve and those you lead.

A successful business is built on a foundation of strong relationships, both inside and outside the organization, and trust is a huge currency in such relationships. I've seen trust produce unparalleled results. Trust is the backbone of high-performing teams. In order to lead with trust, you need to lead with the heart because trust is not operated from the head; it is a function of the heart. But leading with the heart doesn't mean being soft. Leaders with heart can still be demanding, hold people accountable, and have great expectations. Just because you have a great heart doesn't mean you're a pushover, but it does mean having compassion and empathy for the people you lead. So, what does that look like in everyday practice in the trenches of the workplace?

Autonomy, Freedom, and Ownership

Let your team members decide how to do their jobs according to their strengths and talents and how they're naturally wired. There is no right or wrong way of doing things. As long as they are able to deliver quality results on time, that's all that matters. Also, allow them the room to make decisions and mistakes in a way that they feel safe to make mistakes and learn valuable lessons in the process. This helps them take greater ownership of their work.

In terms of flexibility, some people are morning people who like to start their day early, and there are others who prefer starting and ending late. Nothing builds trust more than a leader's ability to be understanding and be flexible when people's lives get crazy and unpredictable. In the end, this gift is worth more than money.

Don't Give Them the Fish; Teach Them How to Fish

Often the biggest parts of my day would be spent in putting out fires. Every time someone from the team would come in with a problem, I'd have to remember and resist the temptation to solve the problem for them. I say resist because it would be so much easier and faster if I just solved it for them. However, this would *not* help them in improving their problem-solving skills. So instead, I would take the opportunity to problem-solve with them and would guide them as needed by asking meaningful questions like "If we had a way to go back in time, say two weeks (when the problem had not begun), what would we do differently so we don't end up where we are today?" Or if anything was possible, "What do you think would be the shortest, fastest, easiest and least expensive way to get to the same or better result?" This approach may seem a bit slow and tedious to anyone looking for a quick fix, but it is most definitely a very effective approach for the long run. Having problem-solved this way over and over for years with my team, I have seen a drastic decrease in the emergence of issues in the first place. When people approach problems with curiosity and a willingness to learn from them, not only does it get easier to solve problems but also to avoid them in the future.

Give People the Gift of Your Time and Attention, Create a Safe Space, and Then Say, "Tell Me More"

I have one rule when it comes to anyone needing my time and attention, whether it's for a professional or a personal reason: I drop everything and listen. Now of course this requires discernment, for example I won't do that for gossip or idle chatter, the topic needs to be meaningful.

Give people the precious gift of your time. Listen attentively to their ideas, opinions, concerns, interests, and personal needs. When it comes to influence, ears over lips. Stop talking; start listening-really listening. Seek your team's input often and on as many topics as possible. Explore different perspectives before enacting new rules or processes. Respect your team members by listening more than speaking. Allow them the freedom to think and be a part of the conversation. When they feel safe, they will ask questions and provide honest and valuable feedback, and you will be able to brainstorm ideas like "How can we be better, more productive, more efficient, etc." Taking the time to listen, understand, appreciate, empathize, and communicate will always add to your ability to lead.

Money Can Buy Valuable Things, Not Invaluable

There was a time when my younger daughter was about three or four years old that she started to notice the power of credit cards. Anytime we went to a store or a restaurant, either my husband or I would simply take out one of the credit cards and pay with it, so she started to assume that she/we could buy anything anytime. All we had to do is use this magical thing and voila, we could have anything we wanted. So, one day my husband and I had to take the time to explain how the world of money worked, in a way that someone her age would understand.

We told her, "Mommy and Daddy don't just *get* money from somewhere, they have to *work* to make money", and that the credit cards don't have magical powers, they need to be paid back with the money we make. Anyway, long story short, pretty sure her little brain grasped the idea. I know this because fast forward to few days later, something interesting happened that confirmed it.

One morning while getting ready for school my older daughter, out of sheer curiosity, happened to ask pointing to a brand name,

"Mom do you work for _____ (brand name)?",

to that my younger daughter very excitedly jumped in to say,

"No silly! She doesn't work for _____ , she works for money!"

Until this day any time I'm reminded of this incident not only does it make me chuckle, but also makes me squirm a tiny bit. The statement "she works for money" may not be inaccurate, but it is definitely incomplete. Yes, we all "work for money" however, what makes work especially enjoyable is when it has a purpose attached to it. As I mentioned earlier, the essence of leadership is influence, and if you can influence people in a positive way and leverage that impact to deliver outstanding results, then it will not only increase your value in the marketplace but also bring you lasting happiness and fulfillment along the way.

CHAPTER 8:

Don't Forget to Connect the dots (E: Evaluate)

E valuation and reflection are a crucial part of the process, they are just as important as taking consistent action. The "process" could be a season, a product launch, a series of projects, an annual review, an evaluation of goals, and the steps involved from start to finish. Constant evaluation during and after the process is critical to sustaining success in the long run. Sometimes people forget to give this step its due importance because they don't think it's as important as the other action-oriented steps. This way of thinking is naïve at best and detrimental at worst.

What's the Collateral Damage?

At a certain point in my career, I was given a very challenging task of leading a brand-new team that was created by merging two separate teams together. Oh, how I *don't* miss the mayhem one bit, the collision of the egos and the constant friction caused because of it, managing people's expectations and the logistical nightmare of figuring out optimal strategies, tactics, and processes all while making sure nothing fell through the cracks! Anyway, for brevity's sake, I'll spare you the details of the challenge. Let's just say to call it a *daunting* task would be an understatement!

That phase of my life was difficult. Although the goals and objectives were being met, the two teams that were merged were finally starting to work harmoniously, the ego clashes were less frequent, projects were being executed on time, samples were being made correctly and on time, and there was steady progress; however, the stress was overwhelming. I came home feeling drained every single day.

So, the *results* were not the problem. It was *what was happening during the process* that was a problem. I remember coming home and wanting to drink a glass of wine, often just to wash the day off.

I'd often semi-jokingly say, "Let me drown my sorrows in fermented grape juice." My typical alcohol consumption of one to two glasses a week was quickly turning into an average of one to two glasses per day. I guess that didn't make me a full-blown alcoholic (I had some wiggle room, so that was good!). But the mere fact that I "needed a drink" on a regular basis became a source of concern for me. I did not want this "collateral damage," i.e. success coming at the price of my peace of mind or health.

I wanted the same results at work but through a more positive and sustainable process. So, I decided to get an outside perspective on how to handle stress. I thought of our CEO. I figured he must have to deal with stress on a constant basis, and he was a very calm and level-headed person, so he must have some systems in place to deal with it. I figured, why not ask him?

So, I did.

He said that he dealt with it by working out regularly. Daily, sometimes twice daily if needed. This was a way of life for him. This tip was incredibly helpful!

At this point in my life, I was not an unhealthy person, but working out daily wasn't exactly a priority for me. I worked out when I *found* the time, which is to say not very regularly. But now, I decided to make a lifestyle change and include a regular workout regimen in it. Fast forward to later. I added exercise to my daily goals and have been a regular ever since. Now, I work out not only to stay healthy and fit but also as a way to manage stress.

Although I'm a huge advocate of the myriad benefits of exercise, as I have shared in the previous chapters, here

I share this story to make a different point, and that point is this: When you are met with an usually big obstacle that's blocking you or slowing you down, digging in your heels and trying to overcome it with sheer brute force may *not* be the smartest approach. Sometimes it might make more sense to take a break, evaluate the process, and try a different approach. A fresh perspective and a new approach could end up being significantly more effective in tackling the situation. This is exactly what I did. Instead of just accepting stress as a part of the process and going for the end results with more determination, I sought out an outside perspective and applied it. This enabled me to get the same results and minimize the "collateral damage" in the process.

Driven individuals, the go-getters, sometimes overlook the fact that this is a very important step in the journey to success. They get caught up in the grind mode and forget that they (and their team as well) could get burnt out in the long run, or the process may be taking away from another important part of their life. Therefore, it's very important to reflect on the process and ensure that you are not only giving it your absolute best but also that the process is not taking a toll on you and others alongside you.

Evaluate your process and the "collateral damage" along the way.

Are you paying too high a price for your results?

If yes, it's time to reassess (Hey, that rhymes! Nice!).

Don't Focus on the Results; Instead, Focus on the Process

People who measure their success only by their results can end up feeling defeated over the long run because often the results may not be what they want. High performers know this. That's the reason they measure their success by asking themselves,

"Did I put in my personal best?"

If the answer is yes, then that's all that matters.

If the answer is no, then they know what to improve upon for the next time to increase their chances for success. They focus on the process, not on the result. This is a really important concept. There are a lot of variables in life, and you can't always control the results. The journey to success is most definitely not linear.

You don't start from point A and end up at Point B (success) in a perfectly straight line. The journey to success actually is similar to that of a jungle gym. Sometimes you go right and then left and backward to be able to go forward.

If you focus on results, you'll ride an emotional roller-coaster. If you constantly evaluate your work exclusively by the outcome you achieve or the result, then you will be ecstatic when everything goes as planned and feel defeated when it doesn't. This will make your life an emotional roller-coaster, and your self-esteem will go up and down in an exhausting and unpredictable manner-not a recipe for a happy life! If you understand and admit to yourself that all you can control is the input you provide in the process, you can pride yourself on good, consistent work regardless of the outcome of any particular result. Focus on your approach, not your results. Learn to look at results as feedback that you need to be aware of. Use your results to tune your approach, but focus on your approach and don't dwell on your results.

Another way to look at it is if you are a driven individual, you will *always* want more. When you reach your current goals, you'll set some new ones, correct? This means at any given moment, you will always be striving towards something in the future. If that's the case and if you only focus on the finish line and hold your breath (metaphorically speaking) until you get there, then you will be holding your breath for your entire life, right? Just some food for thought.

Don't Get Caught Up in Checking Off the Boxes

> *"Strategy without tactics is the slowest route*
> *to victory. Tactics without strategy is*
> *the noise before defeat."*
> – Sun Tzu

Checking off boxes feels amazing! So amazing that the gratifying feeling you get can easily lure you into a "checking off boxes" marathon. When you check off a box, i.e. complete a project, or reach any goal successfully, you get a tremendous high, a feeling of achievement. You want to experience it over and over. It's very seductive, but don't fall prey to it! Hindsight is always 20/20, so use it to look back and connect the dots to see with all the boxes you've been checking off; are they really bringing you closer to your long-term goals, or have they been just exciting activity, not purposeful action?

They say success is a long race made up of a lot of short races put together. So, using that analogy, let's say you put a tactic in motion and end up winning a short race, i.e. achieved a goal. Now look back to make sure that the goal is aligned with your long-term strategy and vision, that it actually helped bring you closer to your big goal. Just because you ran fast and won the short race does not mean you were running in the right direction. Always make sure that the boxes you are checking off, the tactics you are deploying, are actually bringing you closer to your big-picture goal. Tactics are vital to success but only when they are aligned with the long-term strategy. If they're not, then as Sun Tzu said, they are merely the noise before defeat.

When Rubber Hits the Road

My husband and I were trying hard not to laugh at the absurdity of the situation, and at ourselves, as I practiced the awkward breathing techniques I was trying to learn. Our first child was on the way, and we had decided to take a class that would help us get ready for the upcoming labor and childbirth. My husband was instructed to count a certain way, and I was supposed to synchronize my breathing with his counting pace. We had learned many different techniques and other important information at this class. This made us feel prepared for what was coming. We felt, "We got this!"

And then... *labor* happened!

In the beginning, when the contractions began, both of us excitedly started to practice the breathing techniques. He counted, and I paced my breaths. It was almost a sweet and borderline fun experience at first.

But when the pain *really* kicked in, guess what happened?

Ha-ha, all hell broke loose!

Forget trying to relax and taking deep breaths, I was *screaming* so hard that it may have caused an earthquake in Japan.

> *"No plan survives first contact with the enemy.*
> *What matters is how quickly*
> *the leader is able to adapt."*
> – Tim Harford

Another important thing I've learned in business is this: while there is tremendous merit in having a well thought out plan in place, when rubber hits the road, situations often tend to go awry. In that event, what truly counts is your ability to adapt to the situation at hand and make the necessary adjustments. And that adaptation requires an agile mindset.

Get A New Plan

When things don't go as planned, get a new plan. A canceled flight is similar to an employee quitting. It's usually unexpected, sets you back, and produces a ripple effect. What do you do when you get handed an employee resignation? Identify your immediate options. Evaluate which option immediately gets you closer to being on the right track. Then, list the steps you need to take in order to get there, and then put your plan into action immediately. Taking action gets you out of your situation. Dwelling on it doesn't.

Be a Willow, Not an Oak

Be flexible. Roll with the punches. There's a saying that the willow survives because it bends in the wind while the oak tree breaks, standing firm and strong. Therefore, when problems arise, tackle them head-on or go around it, over it, under it, or through it.

Be humble while evaluating the plans you put in motion. Not all of them can be successful-it's virtually impossible.

Even if everything you put into motion is "working," this does not mean it cannot be improved. There's always room for improvement. Therefore, it's crucial to take time to evaluate constantly.

Get Off the Negative Thought Treadmill

Don't go down the rabbit hole of replaying conversations or events that led you to a bad situation or imagining the worst possible outcomes in your head-it isn't helpful. Ask yourself whether your thinking is productive and empowering. If you are actively solving a problem, such as trying to look at the situation from another perspective or trying to find creative ways to solve the problem, keep thinking. If, however, you're wasting your time ruminating, change the channel in your brain immediately. Acknowledge that your thoughts aren't productive and get up and go do something for a few minutes to get your brain focused on something more productive.

> *"If you don't like something, change it.*
> *If you can't change it, change your attitude."*
> – Maya Angelou

CHAPTER 9:

Happiness Delivers Dollar Bills! (R: Rejoice!)

Look around for a moment. The path of success leading to happiness is baked into most people from an early age. That is if you work hard, you will become successful, and once you become successful, then you'll be happy. This is the reason why people are so motivated to become successful. They think if I just get that raise, increase sales, or lose that ten pounds, I'll be happy. And so on. Achieving success and happiness is virtually guaranteed. Is that really true though? Let's explore.

What happens when you reach a big goal of yours?

Do you feel really happy?

Euphoric, even?

For how long?

I mean, how long do you maintain that feeling of euphoria after you reach a big goal? For most people, the answer is "not long." Perhaps a day, a week, or even a month or more. What happens, exactly, when that feeling fades? It is not that you are less pleased to have reached the goal. It is not even that the goal loses some of its meaning. It's merely that part of the joy came from *achieving* something, and once the moment of achievement passes, you are looking for the next goal, the next achievement. In other words, we seldom spend time basking in the satisfaction of what we have achieved. We set another goal and then the next and the next. Sometimes, it may feel that you will just be happy "when..." And then when that condition is met, well, you're not really all that happy, at least not for long. You start looking for the next goal to pursue.

For instance:

A school student thinks, "If I get into a good college, *then* I'll be happy."

When he gets into a good college, he thinks, "If I get a good job, *then* I'll be happy."

When he gets a good job, he thinks, "If I get a promotion, *then* I'll be happy."

When he gets the promotion, he thinks, "If I get into a senior management position, *then* I'll be happy."

The cycle of *"then"* never ends. So clearly, success does not bring happiness (not lasting happiness at least). But here's the awesome part! Groundbreaking research in the fields of positive psychology and neuroscience has conclusively proven that the relationship between success and happiness works the other way around. Thanks to this cutting-edge science with two decades of research backing this up, we now know that *happiness is a key driver and precursor of success*. Happiness and optimism actually fuel performance and achievement, giving people the competitive edge.

In other words, *happiness leads to success*.

One of the reasons for this is happy, positive brains make people more motivated, resilient, creative, efficient, and productive, which boosts performance. This discovery has been confirmed by thousands of scientific studies and Shawn Achor's research on 1,600 Harvard students and dozens of Fortune 500 companies worldwide.

Research also shows that you can do things to be happier. And being happier will make you more successful. And being successful will also make you happier.

So, it's *one big happy loop*!

So, it just makes sense to be happier, but how do you get there? Here are a few ways to increase happiness:

Practice Mindfulness

A study by Harvard psychologists showed that we spend about forty-seven percent of our waking hours thinking about what isn't going on and that this typically makes us unhappy. The solution? To focus on whatever you are doing and the experience you are having in that very moment. In other words, to develop the skill of mindfulness. There are many forms of mindfulness and meditation you can do, information for the same can be readily found online, through apps, books and courses.

Strengthen Your Friendship Circles

Shawn Achor in his book *The Happiness Advantage* talks of the challenges and periods of stress we face. It's how we choose to handle them that's the most telling. Whereas some people choose to retreat within themselves when the going gets tough, the most successful people will instead make time for friends, peers, and family members, always seeking to strengthen their friendship circles. Socializing can add a little something special to your day, so be sure to spend at least an hour catching up with friends, coworkers, neighbors, and family.

Gratitude

We all have ups and downs each day, though when we focus on what we still have, our mood will be enhanced. Most of us have many, many blessings: good health, a loving family, satisfying relationships, an enjoyable career-the list is endless and highly personal. There's also a scientific basis for the statement that gratitude helps increase happiness, demonstrating that it also helps protect you from negativity, stress, depression, and anxiety.

To help you do so, keep a gratitude journal or write a letter thanking someone who has helped you or simply form a daily habit to take a few minutes to actively feel grateful for the people and things in your life. I attended a personal development seminar where I learned a powerful morning ritual called a "priming exercise." One of the things that I do when I do this exercise is to remember three distinct moments that I can be grateful for and actively express feelings of gratitude for them. Every time I do this, it brings me so much joy and happiness to think of the things I'm grateful for, and it adds to my overall sense of wellbeing.

Get Moving and Exercise

A proven way to enhance mood is to stay active and exercise. This is something I covered in Chapter 5, where I elaborated on the myriad benefits of exercise, one of them being a stress reliever. A powerful mantra that sums up the benefits of exercise is "motion creates emotion." Basically, if we move, we will be happy. Even a brisk walk can do wonders for our outlook and daily mood. When adults have around thirty minutes of moderately intense physical activity per day, it has been shown to be an important factor in not only physical health but psychological well-being as well.

The Big "O"

Oxytocin is the hormone of trust and "love." It is a natural calming and feel-good chemical. It connects and bonds people together, and when released, it evokes feelings of contentment, reductions in anxiety, and feelings of calmness and security. Simply touching, hugging, and interacting with loved ones can release oxytocin. Hugging someone you care about or a shoulder rub or a pat on the hand will stimulate your touch receptors, automatically releasing the feel-good brain chemical oxytocin and at the same time decreasing the stress hormones in your body. Hugging will give you these physical benefits plus the added emotional support that comes from connecting with someone you care about. For best results, try sharing a squeeze for around six seconds, the amount of time some research suggests is necessary to really harness the power of a hug.

Smile

This is more than a simple suggestion. It's backed by science. Smiling, even if it's a "fake" smile, can help improve your mood. That's because our brains are hardwired to associate the activation of the face's "smile muscles" with actual happiness. When you turn up the corners of your mouth, your brain physiology will change, and you'll automatically feel better.

Ask for Help When You Need It

There are times when you know you're overwhelmed and will not be able to finish what you started. In addition, you may run into unexpected problems or difficulties while you're working at a task or pursuing a goal and don't know what to do about it. Don't hesitate in asking for help when you need it. In fact, it's a sign of good mental health and a positive attitude that you're comfortable doing so. Another person may be able to provide an invaluable perspective. Similarly, if you're bogged down with financial problems, asking for assistance to overcome them will help you figure out a path to get past this difficulty. Asking for help allows you to get unstuck and move ahead toward your goals. I have a friend who can also be called my life coach. I have often sought her perspective when I've faced with difficult situations, whether they are personal or business-related. Her counsel and sometimes just her presence have been enough to provide the necessary support I needed to effectively problem-solve issues. Sometimes, it's not even what the other person says but just the fact that by engaging in a conversation we are forced to talk about the issues out loud, and in that process, we may come up with solutions that were not apparent to us before.

With so much overwhelming research on happiness and its direct impact on success, it would be naïve of us to put it on the backburner and settle for the hustle and grind mode. The best leaders don't put happiness second. They understand that happiness is the precursor to success and achievement. Also, if they are happier, the people around them will be happier; they will be better communicators and have a bigger impact. Leaders know that if they don't prioritize their happiness, no one else will.

As I shared in Chapter 5, I have a daily habit list where I have purposely chosen activities that help me maintain a positive and empowered state. Many of the activities I have recommended here are included on that list. By creating a daily list, I ensure that I am proactively pursuing my happiness and therefore my success as well.

I recommend the same to you. Make your own list of activities from this list as well as other things that make you happy and make a conscious effort to practice them daily or at least regularly. Once you do, soon you'll start to enjoy the compounded benefits of such a practice.

Why grind your way to success when scientific research tells us to *smile* your way to success!

CHAPTER 10:

What Do Olympians Have in Common?

My daughter and I were playing a board game together. I believe she was around four or five years old at this point. In the middle of the game, she did something that was not allowed per the rules of the game. So, I said to her with a mild frown,

"Hey, Nikki, you can't do that. That's cheating!"

To my surprise, she calmly replied,

"Mom, I'm not trying to cheat. I'm only trying to win."

I still smile every time I think of her reply.

One of the thoughts that occurred to me after I heard this clever comment was,

"Wow, that's actually a genius way to look at things."

And then my mind was flooded with the number of places I could apply this.

Now I could stop paying taxes and, when the IRS asks why I didn't pay my taxes, I'd simply say,

"It's not that I'm not paying taxes. I'm just trying to save money."

Or jump the red light and tell the cops,

"I'm just trying to get to work on time."

Or rob a bank and tell the authorities,

"I'm just trying to get rich."

The list was practically endless.

I don't share this story to establish the importance of cheating while playing board games or breaking rules in our daily lives (Although they both sound tempting! But I digress.) My point is that everyone has a different way of looking at things. They have a certain vantage point, a unique point of view, and when solving a problem, it's always useful to look at it from different angles. It's useful to seek others' perspectives, especially of those whose opinions you can trust.

When I got the idea of writing a book, I acted upon it immediately. I jumped into action. I narrowed down the theme, came up with what the chapters should look like, and even wrote a few chapters. I was quite proud of the progress, and then, all of a sudden, I lost the momentum. Maybe fear crept up, or life took over. I can't say for sure, but I sat on the unfinished book for over a year. I procrastinated. I reasoned. I justified the lack of progress. I had some very solid arguments in my favor.

I worked full-time.

I was a mom of two kids.

Writing a book takes time.

Creativity cannot be forced. Blah blah blah.

It was not until I was honest with myself that I needed an outside perspective from someone I could learn from-someone who had successfully written books and can guide others through the process, someone who would help me get unstuck and reach the finish line and who would not only guide me through the process so it's not more difficult than it needed to be but also hold me accountable, not let me play small. Who would push me to higher standards? So, I did it. I hired a book coach.

Making the decision to hire a coach has been one of the best decisions of my life. It is due to the coaching I received that I was finally able to finish writing my book. Otherwise, it's very likely that my book would still be sitting on my computer as an unfinished manuscript. There are many ways to get to the finish line.

Think about this. If you want to travel somewhere you've never been, you generally look for people who have

gone before you. You make a note of their recommenda-
tions. "Go here; don't go there. Do this. Don't spend your
time on that. Be sure to take this and leave that because you
won't need it…" You do this because you want to make
sure that your trip is smooth and enjoyable. Where you
spend your time and energy on only the good stuff. And
avoid any unnecessary hassles.

The same idea applies when it comes to people who are
successful in their career, business, relationships or performance. It makes sense to seek their point of view. They've
been there and done what we want to do, so it makes a lot
of sense to leverage their knowledge and expertise.

Right now, you may be raring to get to the next level
because you are dissatisfied, or simply because you want
more. Financial worries or feelings of discontent are
causing a strain on your relationships and your lifestyle.
You're not willing to pay this price anymore. You want
to get unstuck and move forward. You look forward to a
future when all this is behind you, when you feel free-
free of worries, free of pain of being stuck, free to live
a life you want. And then you can move onto the next
chapter of your life. You might wonder what it would
be. Well, how life will unfold for you in its next chapter
I cannot say, but what I can say for sure is it is possible.
Everything that you wish and dream of is possible. The
desire to achieve a goal is the first step towards achieving
the goal.

If you are looking to solve problems and you want to make significant change in your life for the better, then know that you don't have to do this alone.

I cannot recommend the value of seeking help enough. Seeking help is a sign of self-worth.

This is what Olympians have in common (other than gorgeous bodies). They have coaches. They have people in their lives guiding them, pushing them, supporting them every step of the way. It would be nearly impossible for any Olympian to complete their journey without this support.

If you have people in your life who have overcome the challenges you are facing, ask them for their guidance. Tell them to walk you through the process. If you don't, then go find people who are experts in the field that you want to succeed in. If you really wish to achieve quality results in less time, then I cannot emphasize the power and effectiveness of coaching enough. Looking back at my journey, if I had to change anything about it, the only thing I would change is seeking the help of coaches sooner and more often.

CHAPTER 11:

Don't Numb the Pain; Feel It, and Then Choose Wisely

L ooking back at my life, one of the best things that I did for myself was to be honest with myself. When I was going through periods of struggle where I was not where I wanted to be in my career and life, I allowed myself to acknowledge that my life was not where I wanted it to be.

I didn't sugarcoat the suffering.

I really allowed myself to feel the pain of being stuck. Every time I was reminded of my problems, by my circumstances, others, or my own thinking, I allowed myself to be moved by it.

I could have found ways to numb the pain. I could've justified my situation and told myself that things were "fine," but I didn't. That would've been a huge disservice to me. Instead, I asked myself questions like these:

- If I saw myself five years into the future at a place similar to where I am now, how would I feel?
- If I was still struggling and facing similar problems as I am now, what effect would they have on my life?"
- What opportunities, in business and in life, would I miss out on if I continued to just run on this endless treadmill without a clear sense of purpose?
- There has to be more to life than this, right?

It was painful to visualize such a scenario. I could not afford to stay stuck. I had to make a change. With this much-needed motivation, I was able to create a massive change in my life. So, I offer you the gift of such questions:

- Where do you see yourself five years from now?
- Is the place similar to where you are now?
- If yes, how does it make you feel if things haven't changed much?
- What opportunities for growth or improving the quality of your life could you possibly miss if you stay stuck?

Is this as painful for you as it was for me?

If yes, then I want you to realize that even though initiating change can be hard, it's not nearly as hard as the pain caused from being stuck. The pain that comes from not living a life you want to live is much harder to bear. The feeling of not being fulfilled and not being able to live up to your potential can crush your soul. A life where you constantly worry about the present and the future can be draining.

When you *know* in your heart that you can do more, make more, and be more, you achieve more! So, I'd like to remind you that you don't need to settle because you don't have to. My journey is living proof that you can achieve success even when the odds are not in your favor.

A world of possibilities will open up when you overcome your obstacles. You will not only enjoy what you already have but also reach for more because you'll know from your own experience that it's possible. In my journey, not only did I overcome the seemingly insurmountable problems and come out stronger on the other side, but I also found a renewed purpose in life. I found a purpose that's greater than me, the purpose to share my message with the world. This purposefulness gives me more joy and fulfillment than I have ever felt pursuing anything else in my entire career. I feel *secure* about my financial future!

I know that, come what may, my future is safe, and this feeling allows me to fully enjoy my present. I wish the same level of security, joy, and fulfillment for you.

My wish for you is to live a life where you do not have to settle.

That you recognize the power inside of you.

That you play big with your life.

Push the boundaries of what's possible and bring out the greatness that's waiting to come out from inside of you.

I wish that you create a positive ripple effect in the world, and you infect everyone around you with positivity, hope, and joy. When your loved ones look at you and your victorious journey, it gives them hope and the courage to pursue their own.

I wish that you apply your courage and self-assurance to everything you touch and also allow yourself to be touched by love, inspiration, and grace.

I wish you accept your greatness wholeheartedly and allow you to shine your light upon the world and do so without ever feeling apologetic for being as magnificent as you are because now you have realized that by doing so, you redefine what's possible for others as well as give them permission to dream and play big.

I wish your curiosity gets bigger than your fears every time.

I wish you have boundless gratitude for this beautiful miracle called life. I wish your life is one big, daring adventure. I wish you this metamorphosis, this transformation that turns you into a butterfly.

I wish you risk being seen in all of your beauty, again and again.

Above all, I wish you love. Unconditional, abundant love.

My Life-Altering Question

There comes a time in life when we ask ourselves a question that could prove to be life-altering-something that could put us in a state of catharsis.

Some time ago, before the onset of my journey of transformation and growth, I watched one of Tony Robbins' speeches. It was about elephants in the circus. He talked about why it is that a giant elephant that has enough power to rip the tent and create havoc in a single moment acts as timid as he does and ends up dancing to the tunes of his instructor. The reason for this has to do with how he has been conditioned.

When he was a baby and not as powerful, he was tied down with a big rope around his neck, with which he fought and fought and fought until one day something snapped inside of him. He stopped fighting and resigned to the fact that he was powerless. That became his identity. He was conditioned to believe that the rope was more powerful than him. He accepted it as his reality and that made him lose touch with his magnificent self (Unfortunate!).

Later, as I was reflecting on this speech, I had an aha moment, and a life-altering question popped into my head. I asked myself,

"What if I am that elephant as well?

Did I also just give in to societal conditioning, the lies, and start believing in a story that was not true?

Did I, just like the elephant, also unknowingly give up my power?"

The answer (very reluctantly) came back as "probably yes."

I had bought into the lie…

A lie about the limits of what one can achieve.

A lie about success and what it takes to achieve it.

A lie about what is true happiness and how to pursue it.

A lie about greatness and how only a few are destined to be great.

And many more lies like these…

As I reflected some more and went further down that rabbit hole, I realized that it wasn't just me. Every one of us is that elephant who is destined to be great, who has abundant power but probably doesn't realize that she has it (yet). However, once we discover and acknowledge our infinite power, we can become unstoppable.... and then, nothing is impossible!

Sometimes when I look back at my journey and see where I was a short few years ago and how far I've come, I get overwhelmed with joy and gratitude. I get emotional when I acknowledge not only the growth in my career, relationships, and overall wellbeing but most importantly as a person. Because I pushed my ego aside and allowed myself to learn and grow *so* much in the past few years, I was able to reinvent myself as a person. I became more valuable to myself and those around me by acquiring so many new skills and positive tools for business and life.

This renewed skillset, attitude, and confidence in my abilities gives me a swagger, a strong sense of security, and a feeling of self-assurance that runs deep. Nothing can ever touch it-it's mine to keep because I earned it.

Besides, I'm not done yet. I will continue to grow until the day I die. Now, I feel unstoppable because I know that I could possibly face more obstacles in life, but I am bigger than any obstacle!

You are too.

In closing, I leave you with one of my most favorite quotes by Marianne Williamson:

"Our deepest fear is not that we are inadequate.
Our deepest fear is that we are powerful beyond measure.
It is our light, not our darkness that most frightens us.
We ask ourselves, who am I to be brilliant,
gorgeous, talented, fabulous?
Actually, who are you not to be? You are a child of God.
Your playing small does not serve the world."

Acknowledgments

T hank you to Angela Lauria and The Author Incubator's team, as well as to David Hancock and the Morgan James Publishing team for helping me bring this book to print.

Thank You!

Thank you so much for reading!
I would love to learn more about your journey and success in your career. Please keep in touch.
I'm most active on Facebook and Instagram.

Facebook: https://www.facebook.com/vandy.verma.1234/

Instagram: https://www.instagram.com/vandy.verma/

About the Author

Vandy Verma is a best-selling author, entrepreneur, mom of two, avid life-long learner, stubborn optimist, and most of all, a dreamer.

It is her life's mission to help people realize that there is a L.E.A.D.E.R. inside each and every one of us waiting to be discovered. By becoming that leader, you can go from feeling unsure to secure in practically any area of your life, whether it's your financial future, career, business, or life itself!

Vandy is passionate about helping motivated individuals achieve breakthroughs and get to the next level in their personal and professional lives. She is excited to bring decades of experience from the business world and share the countless game-changing insights that she has acquired as a senior business leader in corporate America with her book, coaching programs, seminars, and speaking engagements.

Vandy lives in Long Island, New York, with her husband and two children, aka, her life coaches. When she's not working with driven individuals and helping them achieve their dreams, she likes to spend time reading books, traveling, playing tennis, swimming, meditating, running, singing, dancing, hiking, trying new cuisines, climbing trees, having deep and meaningful conversations with people, watching movies, learning new skills, and making memories.